Endorsements for
8 Ways to Wellbeing for Recovering People

People are saying …..

"Everyone begins recovery work hoping in their heart that they can stop using drugs and alcohol for good. But, addiction doesn't happen in the heart; it happens in the brain. This is where Dr. Weedn's workbook comes in … providing an excellent recipe for healing the brain and optimizing mental and physical health. We'll use it as part of our comprehensive treatment program."

—Roy Duprez, M.S. Ed., Owner, *Back2Basics Outdoor Adventures*

"When addiction sets in, the person and their history fall into an abyss of pain and suffering. Dr. Weedn's workbook offers a guide to exit the darkness and remain sober, with a no-nonsense, kind and loving message, and realistic invitation to rebuild health and enjoy life again. This is a must read for those healing from addiction of any kind."

—Ana Nogales, Ph.D., Founder, *Casa de la Familia* and *Nogales Psychological Counseling*

"This is FABULOUS! It is simple, elegant, and powerful. I would love to see this as the meat and potatoes – sorry the tofu and veggies of every treatment program."

—Michele Saloner, Ph.D.

"Healing from addiction is very hard work. Revisiting childhood traumas, reconnecting with long denied feelings and emotions we have spent a lifetime eschewing, and building a life that supports health and intimacy, these are not small tasks. This workbook will give a structure you can lean into and rely on to support you in your healing. You can rely on its guidance and wisdom when the going gets tough and it will get tough. Dr. Weedn has valuable insight into this work and her workbook can become an important part of your healing journey."

—Patricia Ravitz, MFT, *President of the Marin Chapter of the California Association of Marriage and Family Therapists*

"*8 Ways to Wellbeing for Recovering People* is a package of great enlightenment for the human body and is grounded in practicality."

—Lama Tenzin Choegyal, Humanitarian, Tibetan Buddhist Monk

"This book is a reflection of the deep caring Dr. Weedn has for her patients, and is complimentary to her clinical work. She is always seeking the best for her patients and anyone who wants to live a fruitful and peaceful life should read this workbook and follow her directions."

—Laila Elkeeb, M.D.

8 Ways to Wellbeing
For Recovering People

8 Ways to Wellbeing
For Recovering People

By Sonnee D. Weedn, Ph.D.

Copyright © 2019 by Sonnee D. Weedn

All rights reserved. No part of this publication may be reproduced, distributed, or transmitted in any form or by any means, including photocopying, recording, or other electronic or mechanical methods, without the prior written permission of the publisher, except in the case of brief quotations embodied in critical reviews and certain other noncommercial uses permitted by copyright law. For permission requests, write to the publisher, addressed "Attention: Permissions Coordinator," at the address below.

Disclaimer: This book is meant to supplement, not replace, proper medical advice of physicians. The reader should regularly consult a physician in matters relating to his/her health and particularly with respect to any symptoms that may require diagnosis or medical attention.

Printed in the United States of America

ISBN Paperback: 978-0-9832776-2-0

Interior Book Design: Ghislain Viau, info@creativepublishingdesign.com
Cover Art: Lisa Wenrick, lisa@lwenrick.com

8 Ways to Wellbeing for Recovering People

Mission Statement: To inform, inspire, support, and empower all people suffering or recovering from any form of addiction. This workbook is intended to provide an interactive means to educate and enable the reader to create and sustain behavior change strategies and optimize health, wellness and the resilience of recovery for a lifetime.

Acknowledgments

8 Ways to Wellbeing was developed by Roger Walsh, M.D., PhD. I thank him for encouraging me to create this workbook. www.drrogerwalsh.com, https://en.wikipedia.org/wiki/Roger_Walsh

Rev. George McLaird's advice, input and contributions were invaluable in moving this project forward. His influence in my life and thinking is pervasive.

Angeles Arrien, Ph.D. was responsible for introducing me to Dr. Walsh and his work, and encouraging me to collaborate with him in some fashion.

Jan Kingaard provided invaluable guidance and encouragement throughout the writing of this workbook. Her research, organizational skills, and editing expertise are invaluable. In addition, she has been my friend since Junior High School. Old friends are the best friends!

Table of Contents

Foreword xiii

Preface xv

Introduction: Let's Get Started xix

Directions for Using This Workbook xxiii
    Lifestyle Survey xxiv
    Getting Started xxvi

Chapter 1: Nutrition: You Are What You Eat 1

Chapter 2: Exercise: We Are Made to Move! 19

Chapter 3: Relaxation: Breathe In, Breathe Out…Aaah 29

Chapter 4: Recreation: Fun is Fun-damental 45

Chapter 5: Relationships: We Influence & Need Each Other 57

Chapter 6: Time in Nature: A Source of Healing 79

Chapter 7: Giving Back: Giving the Gift of Generosity 93

Chapter 8: Spirituality: "We Came to Believe …." 103

Final Words 127

References 129

About the Author 139

Appendix A – Worksheets 143

Appendix B – Additional Resources 167

Foreword

Science and technology have changed the world in ways both beneficial and problematic. On one hand, they have showered us with technological miracles that make life longer, healthier, and easier. Yet they have also created innumerable unforeseen problems, and put dangerous technologies—from bombs to drugs—in unwise hands.

One specific blessing and curse is the ability to create more, and ever more potent, drugs. Modern drugs have saved and prolonged countless lives. Yet they have also destroyed countless others as humans have learned how to better distill alcohol, refine old drugs, synthesize new ones, and administer them in novel ways such as through needles.

The result? Millions of deaths and hundreds of millions of addicts every year. In the United States, narcotics currently get most of the press. However, they are only part of the problem. According to the World Health Organization, worldwide, some 250,000 people die annually from illegal drug use (mainly amphetamines and narcotics), over three million die from alcohol abuse, and seven million from nicotine. And let's face it: things may get worse as further drugs become available.

What's the cause? Of course, there are many. However, debate usually polarizes into three camps: moral, medical, and social. From the moral perspective, addiction is a personal failing; from the medical, a disease; and from the social perspective, addiction reflects social factors such as poverty, inequality, and harsh life conditions.

There is also a fourth perspective: a spiritual or contemplative one. This sees craving as a symptom of our usual painfully constricted egoic identity, and its complications such as alienation. Importantly, it recognizes that we can become addicted to anything—money, power, status possessions, people, and more. Drugs are just an extreme example.

People's approach to treatment follows from their perspective. For moralists, an appropriate response is criminalization. Medical people suggest that addiction requires medical and psychological treatment. Those emphasizing a social perspective urge that we alleviate causative social conditions such as poverty and inequality, while contemplatives recommend adding contemplative practices such as meditation or yoga.

The United States has largely gone with the morality/criminalization approach, and has waged a "war on drugs" which has been America's longest and perhaps least successful war. Other countries such as Portugal have emphasized medical approaches and been more, though by no means completely, successful.

So is there any intervention that everyone, of every belief and political persuasion, could agree on? There is, and it is to help people change their lifestyle.

Why lifestyle changes? Because research shows that therapeutic lifestyle changes (or TLCs)—such as changing one's diet, regular exercise, relaxation, fostering supportive relationships, and service to others—can be enormously beneficial for both mental and physical health and well-being. For example, a good exercise program can sometimes be as effective in healing and preventing depression as can antidepressant medications or psychotherapy.

Therapeutic lifestyle changes can also help with addiction and reduce the risk of relapse. Of course, TLC's are not the whole answer; no one thing is. However, they are a very valuable and under utilized answer.

We can therefore be very grateful to Sonnee Weedn, who has distilled lifestyle interventions into this practical workbook. For people wrestling with addiction or in various stages of recovery, this book with its systematic introduction to therapeutic lifestyle changes can be life changing, and perhaps even life saving.

Of course, lifestyle changes and recovery require work – every effective treatment does. But for those who would like additional support for their recovery, and to feel better and healthier at the same time, the lifestyle program in this book may be what you're looking for. I certainly hope you find it helpful.

Roger Walsh MD, PhD, DHL.
Professor of Psychiatry, University of California at Irvine

Preface

Recovery From Anything

Recovery from chemical dependency of any kind or process addictions (gambling, compulsive shopping, sexual compulsivity, codependency, to name a few) is complicated, because addiction touches most every aspect of one's life. Almost always professional help is indicated to break free. What are frequently overlooked in most behavioral health treatment settings are the very real changes in mental, as well as physical health that can take place when particular attention is paid to therapeutic lifestyle changes, which I will refer to as TLCs.

Optimizing Your Recovery

If you are opening this workbook, you have made a decision to optimize your recovery work and create a program to enhance your general health and wellbeing. A decision about making recovery a way of life is a decision to improve your physical and mental health, in general. But, I hope it is the beginning of your learning about the various aspects of wellness that provide the best opportunities to live well in the long run. This program is evidence-based. My mentor, Dr. Roger Walsh at The University of California at Irvine, spent years researching the aspects of daily life and lifestyle that lead to overall health and wellbeing, and I have simply adapted his findings to support recovering people.

For you to optimize your recovery or begin your recovery program, be it from chemical dependency or process addictions, your good intentions and will alone are not sufficient to assure you of success in achieving and maintaining your recovery.

Successful Long-Term Recovery

Successful, long-term recovery takes a realistic, personalized, informed plan, the intension and will to follow the plan meticulously *and* an experienced person or community who supports your recovery. Accountability to another person or a group will prove helpful in this endeavor. I believe that our greatest healing takes place in community. So, I hope you will consider embarking on this program with a friend or group who can help you set reasonable goals and be accountable for them. As they say, "Progress, not Perfection."

This workbook contains all of the ingredients for you to create that realistic, personalized and informed plan to be used in addition to your treatment program, possible 12 Step membership and therapy. When used in conjunction with a support group of some sort or your therapist, it is an extremely powerful tool.

Identifying Your Support Person or Group

Because I have suggested using this workbook in conjunction with a therapist, a group or a friend, I hope you will identify that support right now. As soon as you finish reading this paragraph, begin your search for the right person or group to assist you. Then, in conjunction with them, formulate your plan. Please write the name/names of your support person(s) in the space below. If environments or situations change, please update this area as needed.

Congratulations! You are about to embark on a fabulous healing journey.

People Who Support Me Getting Healthy

Name	Telephone	Email	Relationship

Introduction: Let's Get Started

Begin Well

It is important to begin well, and setting clear intention is a good way to start. Please sit back in your seat for a moment and reflect on what you hope to have achieved in your recovery by the time one year has passed. Think about what you hope your life is like. Close your eyes for just a minute now and get an image of yourself healthy in every possible way. Good! Now that you have that picture in your mind's eye, write a brief paragraph of what you wish for yourself one year from now. Be very, very specific and make sure that whatever you are intending is measurable.

Now that you have an idea or an image in mind, write a few goals that will help you achieve that image and the reasonable length of time you believe it will take you to achieve those goals.

Personal Goal	Time to Achieve Goal
1)	
2)	
3)	
4)	
5)	

Now write down what the main benefits will be to you as you pursue these goals. Refer specifically to each one that you have written.

Personal Goal	Benefits of Pursuing Goal
1)	
2)	
3)	
4)	
5)	

Great! Now write a bit about how you might sabotage these goals (we all have that saboteur in us, you know). When we know ourselves well, we know some of the ways in which we might get off track.

Now write some ideas about what you will do to get yourself back on track when and if the Saboteur has taken over. Be specific.

What Sabotages Personal Goal	How to Get Back On Track
1)	
2)	
3)	
4)	
5)	

Most people enjoy being rewarded in some way when they can eliminate detrimental habits and behaviors, and replace them with health promoting ones. What would be some healthy ways that you can reward yourself when you are on track with your goals? List at least five possibilities.

1. _____

2. _____

3. _____

4. _____

5. _____

Great! This section where you set intention and examined your process a bit is now complete. Before continuing, use the space below to draw a picture symbolizing your mental well-being. This can be realistic or symbolic ... you choose. Use crayons or colored pencils to really make your picture come to life!

Directions for Using This Workbook

Recovery is a Lifelong Process

Recovery is a lifelong process. Exposing the human brain and body to the toxicity of street drugs or excessive prescription drugs or alcohol is quite harmful. And, the so-called process addictions (codependency, shopping, gambling, sexual compulsivity, eating disorders, etc.) are generally a response to stress or trauma in the absence of healthier coping strategies. Either way, the brain and body will require time and attention to recover. Beyond the initial achievement of sobriety, which is no small thing, it will be important to achieve and maintain a sense of wellbeing to guard against relapse. That's the point of this workbook. It is not your fundamental program of recovery, but an adjunct program to help you create an overall sense of wellbeing through *therapeutic lifestyle changes*, which I will refer to as TLCs.

This is not meant to take the place of psychotherapy or properly supervised medication, if that is necessary. But, these TLCs are a proven way to reduce some of the psychological symptoms and suffering that often accompany addiction, such as feelings of anxiety and depression, agitation, anger, trouble concentrating, as well as low energy and poor self-esteem. Often, these TLCs reduce or eliminate the need for psychiatric medication and head off future problems such as relapse, dementia and other mind/body issues.

You are either just starting this process or have decided to enhance your program of recovery by learning about and doing more to attain and maintain mental health and wellbeing. That's great! Since the importance of lifestyle for mental health is little appreciated in our culture, and only a small minority of mental health professionals emphasize TLCs, I am excited to share this information with you.

So, let's take a look at the **8 Ways to Wellbeing**, and what science and research tell us about living wisely and well, with recovering people in mind!

1. **Nutrition:** You are What You Eat
2. **Exercise:** We are Designed to Move
3. **Relaxation:** Take a Deep Breath In, and Then … Just Let It Go
4. **Recreation:** Fun is Fun-Damental
5. **Relationships:** We Influence Each Other and We Need Each Other
6. **Nature:** Time in Nature is a Source Of Healing
7. **Giving Back:** Giving the Gift of Generosity
8. **Spirituality:** "We Came to Believe …"

Lifestyle Survey

I'll start by asking you to assess yourself in each of the *8 Ways to Wellbeing* that have been identified. Fill out the following questionnaire to determine your level of comfort and participation in each of the categories identified. When you have completed the questionnaire, you will have a better understanding of where you stand and what your areas of strength and challenge are. At that point, you can choose one or more areas that challenge you, read the introductory material on each, and make your action plan to introduce or enhance that area of recovery. This is also a good time to share this with your identified support person, therapist or group.

~ *8 Ways to Wellbeing for Recovering People*: Lifestyle Survey ~

Lifestyle factors are critical to the physical and mental health of recovering people (and everyone else, for that matter). For each of the Therapeutic Lifestyle Changes (TLCs) listed, please indicate your guestimate (on average) of how many hours or minutes per week you spend on each, and how many hours or minutes you would like to spend on each.

Directions for Using This Workbook

Name _____ Male or Female (circle one)

Date of Birth _____ Today's Date _____

8 Ways to Wellbeing	Actual Hours Per Week	Desired Hours Per Week
Nutrition (healthy choices)		
Exercise (sports, walking, yoga, gym, etc.)		
Giving Back (contributions, altruism)		
Relationships (family, friends, 12 Step meetings)		
Relaxation/Mindfulness (fight or flight vs. rest and digest)		
Recreation and Play (music, dance, games, movies, sober fun)		
Time in Nature (time spent outdoors)		
Spiritual Development (care of your soul)		

Other Obstacles to Optimal Health

It is often true that recovering people have other health challenges that should be addressed at some point. Though it is not the purpose of this workbook to address these, I would like you to make note of any other issues you identify that are obstacles to you obtaining optimal health. Just identify them and write a few notes to yourself about how and when you would like to address them. I thought of a few possibilities, but add whatever you can think of for yourself.

Sleep Hygiene – Are you able to consistently get 7-8 hours of sleep a night? If not, this is problematic and should be addressed. Don't wait too long. Try to avoid all screen activity and bright lights one hour before bedtime. Set a regular bedtime and wake-up time and try to maintain it. This should help sleep problems you may encounter. Make some notes about your sleep habits. If you have been taking sleep aids of any kind, consult your doctor or health care professional about weaning off of them.

Smoking, Vaping, Smokeless Tobacco – You don't need me to tell you that smoking, vaping, and other forms of smoking (anything), and smokeless tobacco are all extremely detrimental to your health. What is your plan for cessation of all smoking, vaping and/or chewing? Make some notes about this and share with your support person(s). Yes, I know it is hard! But, it is vitally important and you will be so glad you did this. I also know that there are social aspects to smoking and vaping, but I think you can learn to socialize without hurting yourself! Be a leader, not a follower! Set the tone for your recovery!

Getting Started

You've taken the Inventory to assess your areas of strength among the *8 Ways*, and your areas of challenge. Just because you found strengths doesn't mean you don't need to read the material I have provided for you. In fact, it might be wise to pick one of your areas of relative strength and read over the material to see how you might build on this strength and amplify it. Sometimes it's easier to get started on a project with something you have relative comfort with. In any case, all *8 Ways* are presented in no particular order of importance. You can choose wherever you like to start. Read over the material and possibilities for implementing them. Then, create some goals to incorporate this therapeutic lifestyle change into your everyday life. Write them in the spaces provided and keep track using the daily tracker pages in Appendix A. Let's go!

MY GOALS FOR LIFESTYLE CHANGES

CHAPTER 1
Nutrition: You are What You Eat

*Our food should be our medicine
and our medicine should be our food.*
—Hippocrates

The Reasons Why

There is truth in the claim that you are what you eat. After all, the miracle of our bodies is that they use whatever food we provide for them and turn it into energy and the building blocks to renew our cells. The relationship you have with food has a large impact on your physical health, as well as your mental health.

As we now know, we cannot separate mind and body. What affects the body, affects the mind, and vice versa. What is obvious is that if you want to restore your body, with your brain being a vital part of that body, improving your diet and general nutrition is vitally important. Some might say that paying attention to our nutrition is a high form of self-care and self-love. But, most importantly, in this chapter, I am NOT talking about diet, as in "a diet." I am talking about diet and nutrition as a lifestyle commitment. There is a big difference and I am hoping you will adopt the suggestions I will make, which are general ones, as a lifestyle that is fundamental to recovery and general health. If you want further refinement to your own eating and nutrition, I advise consulting with a registered dietician or nutritionist to help customize your eating plans, based on your particular needs. In this chapter, I will offer some general guidelines and information and help you take stock of where you are now and what might be possible for you to begin to improve this area of wellbeing.

Write a few sentences here about how you would evaluate your overall nutrition.

_____

_____

_____

_____

Do you eat "fast food?" _____ How often? _____

Do you eat fresh fruit? _____ What kind? _____

How often? _____ Organic? _____

Do you eat fresh vegetables? _____ How often? _____

What kind? _____ Organic? _____

Do you eat processed food (most anything that comes in a package or that does not resemble its original form)? _____

_____

How often? _____ What kinds? _____

_____

_____

Do you eat red meat (beef, lamb, pork, etc.,)? _____

How often? _____

Organically raised? _____ Factory farmed? _____

Do you know the difference between the two? _____

Do you eat fish or shellfish? _____ How often? _____

Do you check to make sure it was line caught as opposed to farmed? _____

Sustainably managed? _____

Do you drink diet or sugary sodas? _____ How often? _____

Do you drink "energy" drinks? _____ How many and how often? _____

_____

_____

I am not suggesting that you have to be rigid about your diet and nutrition. I **do** want you to begin thinking about the food you eat, how it is sourced and its impact on you. I want you to read labels on food that comes in a can or package of any kind to consider if there are artificial coloring or chemicals in them and whether those things are good for your nutrition. If you eat animal protein (and, I do) I want you to consider the means by which the animal was raised and slaughtered, because this will determine what that animal was made of before it became part of you. If it was factory raised, it is likely full of hormones, and antibiotics that are not good for you to consume. Also, factory farmed animals are generally kept in inhumane conditions and are quite stressed and therefore full of cortisol (stress hormones) that are unhelpful to your general health and wellbeing.

Likewise, I want you to be aware that buying organic fruits, vegetables, and meat and chicken, as well as line caught fish, means that you will have less exposure to toxins in pesticides, and antibiotics and hormones given to animals.

It is no secret that when the body, and therefore, the brain, have been exposed to toxic chemicals, they will begin to break down in ways that may not be noticeable at first or to the untrained eye. But, when chemically dependent people are given physicals that include evaluating vitamin and mineral deficiencies, as well as overall health of the body, they are often found to be less than optimally healthy and often deficient in important vitamins and minerals.

Also, if the physical includes cognitive testing to determine the health of the brain, there will often prove to be cognitive slippage due to a combination of the toxic exposure of whatever chemicals (including alcohol) have been ingested, as well as generally poor nutrition. The good news is that the body and brain, given proper support, will usually be able to heal themselves and return to a state of health. Whatever support you can provide, through good nutrition will eventually lead to more physical strength, stamina and general robustness, and, also improved brain function.

Often, the images of a life in recovery are not very compelling. My colleague, Tommy Rosen says, "The images of recovery we have been shown in books, television shows and movies depict very sick people who do not seem to be getting better. In fact, often when you go to 12-Step meetings, everyone is smoking, and drinking lots of coffee." He doesn't mention the intense craving for sugar that often comes in early recovery, but you can observe that, too.

I am not criticizing ... just noticing. Everyone has to start somewhere in recovery and just stopping the drinking and using is a great beginning. But, I am hoping for more than that in this workbook! I am advocating for optimal health and wellbeing, to ensure ongoing sobriety and recovery, and that takes time, effort and commitment.

Sadly, the advertising, factory farming, restaurant and packaged goods industries in Western society are geared toward encouraging unhealthy choices. Everyday you are bombarded with ads encouraging you to consume sugar, alcohol, nicotine, and fast food in the never-ending search for what the food industry calls the "bliss point" of "eatertainment" through "hyper-eating" enormous portions and empty calories. Unfortunately you can never get enough of what you do **not** really need -- but you can certainly ruin your health and life-style trying. Let's do better!

Irregular eating, fast food and generally poor diet tend to go hand in hand with substance abuse. Chemically dependent people are typically more interested in their drug of choice than they are in the food they choose. Research shows connections between nutrition, behavior and addiction recovery and the important implications that must be addressed. For example, drug and/or alcohol addiction may cause a person to forget what it is like to be hungry and instead mistake this feeling for a drug craving. **Read that sentence again!** It was important!

Many of the diseases associated with alcoholism are caused by nutritional deficiencies. This includes alcoholic liver disease, and alcoholic dementia. The American Dietetic

Association states that, "Nutrition intervention in treatment and recovery from chemical dependency is imperative. Many debilitating nutritional consequences result from drug and alcohol abuse. Chronic nutrition impairment causes serious damage to the liver and brain, which reinforces the craving for more drugs and alcohol and perpetuates the psychological aspect of the addiction. During treatment, efforts are concentrated on the physical recovery, providing adequate nutrition to replete and heal the brain, liver and digestive system. Nutrition makes a difference in the rate and quality of physical recovery, which prepares people to function at a higher level in treatment --- cognitively, mentally, and socially. Improved nutritional status can make treatment more effective, while reducing drug and alcohol craving, thereby preventing relapse."

Once detox is complete, it is vital to begin the process of rebuilding the brain and body through good nutrition. So, what follows is the general information I have gathered to get you started. If you have an eating disorder or other nutritional concerns, be sure to consult your registered dietitian, nutritionist or health care provider.

Americans spend more than 40% of their food budget on meals outside of the home. Eating out can be convenient, but it's also expensive and the food is typically high in calories, and often contains high amounts of sodium (salt) and sugar. The average restaurant meal has as much as 60% more calories than a homemade meal. Studies show that when we are presented with more food, we eat more food. Knowing the actual ingredients of what is being served in a fast food outlet or other restaurant meal is almost impossible.

How often do you eat out rather than preparing food at home? _____

In the restaurants you frequent, are the calorie contents and ingredients in the dishes listed on the menu? _____

What are your favorite places to eat out if you do? _____

Are they establishments that will support good nutrition and health?

If they do support good nutrition, well, great. If not, any ideas about where else you might eat out that would be healthier and where you can actually discern what the ingredients are?

Make nutrition and health a priority and choose wisely. Go to places that support your goal to maintain a health-enhancing lifestyle and avoid those that undermine your program. In addition, remember that restaurants will generally accommodate any requests you make, so ask for what you want.

So, what exactly is a healthy diet? There have been so many crazy diet schemes and fads in the media that it is hard to know what to do. I have made some general recommendations here, but please consult your physician, nutritionist or other medical adviser before taking my word for it. And, understand that these are very general guidelines.

- Lots of fresh vegetables, organic, if possible
- Healthy fats, such as olive oil
- Fresh fruit, organic, if possible
- Meat, eggs and dairy, raised in as close to the animal's natural environment as possible (grass fed cows, pasture raised chickens, etc.)
- Limit processed foods. If it comes in a package, read the ingredients list carefully and avoid if there are ingredients whose names you don't recognize (often chemicals and dyes)
- No Fast Food,
- Little or no sugar (or sugar substitutes), artificial sweeteners, preservatives, or other ingredients you don't recognize or have trouble pronouncing
- Whole grains (no white flour)

I know, I know! It sounds challenging! And, it is! Again, I'll quote that A.A. aphorism, *"Progress, not perfection."* Make some small changes and see how that goes, tackling one nutritional habit at a time. For example, make a goal of eating two or three fresh fruits each day. Track it for awhile until it is a habit and see how it goes. When you are doing that consistently, choose another nutritional goal to add to the first one.

As much as possible, take the time to prepare and eat meals at home. Don't inhale your food standing up or on the go. Focus on the pleasures of eating. You are encouraged to cook with family or friends, eat together, talk together, and make mealtime a relaxing experience. Eating together helps build close relationships, too.

Possible Actions for Implementation

Take charge of what you put in your body. Focus on what you need and the foods that will supply you with the nutrients required to optimize thinking and energy to do what you want to do. Describe what you typically eat and drink in a day, including any supplements you take:

Morning	
Afternoon	
Evening	
Snacks	

Are you? underweight _____ just right for your age/height _____ overweight _____

An aspect of physical fitness is good nutrition and physical fitness is defined as your mind and body's ability to function efficiently and effectively in activities, to be healthy, to resist disease, to have endurance, and to recover normally. On a scale of 0 to 5, are you physically fit (5) or easily fatigued and unhealthy (0)?

Circle your level of fitness right now: 0   1   2   3   4   5

This chapter will help you know how to incorporate healthier eating habits into your life. These habits can further strengthen your body, improve brain function and help you overcome drug/alcohol cravings. The skills you learn and practice will help you keep your body as healthy and disease-free as possible to support recovery.

People in early recovery have often neglected to take care of the body. Being nutrition-savvy and eating a healthier diet will help your body recover. Sometimes feelings of fatigue, depression or anxiety are actually caused by early signs of malnutrition. Your food habits can bring on cravings, heart disease, stroke, some types of cancer, diabetes, and osteoporosis. Researchers exploring both neuro-circuitry and nutrition have found that eating well can not only help you feel better, but promote clearer thinking and general brain health.

If you have food allergies or sensitivities, please list them here.

_____

_____

_____

_____

_____

Write about your **attitude** toward making some changes to your diet and nutrition.

_____

_____

_____

_____

_____

_____

_____

Being chemically dependent can change your appetite and it may take a while to get your appetite back or get it in check once it does come back. If you are alcoholic, you may notice an intense craving for sugar. This is common. If you don't feel like eating, don't force yourself to eat a lot at one time. Have small meals that include foods that look good to you, and eat regularly to maintain your blood sugar levels and your energy.

Are you experiencing sugar cravings or other cravings that are unhelpful? What about cravings for soda pop? Understand that diet drinks are harmful to the brain and body and are to be avoided, so include those in your discussion.

Do you overeat when stressed, bored, upset or tired? If you find that you're using food as a coping or control strategy, then try to problem solve using other strategies, such as relaxation, recreation, exercise or time in nature. Make small changes over a period of days, weeks and months so you'll stay with your program.

Write about any tendency to overeat or under-eat.

Eating in a healthy manner does not mean sacrificing taste and the pleasure that delicious food brings. However, food manufacturers use persuasive ads and alluring packaging to keep their processed foods tapping into your cravings. These foods contain chemical compounds that stimulate the brain's secretion of opiate-like, "feel-good" chemicals like dopamine, which drive cravings for sugary, salty or fatty foods. If your stomach is growling at the thought of potato chips, mocha latte grandé, cola and cookies, give yourself three weeks without them, and your tastes will change and you probably won't want the food as much. Select the freshest items available at the grocery store, fruit stand, fish market, specialty store, organic food cooperative--or, grow your own. Farmer's Markets are a wonderful place to shop for fresh fruits and vegetables, and sometimes meat raised and killed by the farmer you buy it from, and fish from the people who fished for it. Knowing where your food comes from is a powerful habit to adopt.

To keep your energy balanced all day, nutritionists typically advise three meals and two healthy snacks between meals each day. This will help keep you from feeling tired, and prevent mood swings and cravings. Eating well can enhance your ability to perform tasks, preserve cognitive functions, and may reduce symptoms of depression and anxiety.

Make a list here of healthy snacks that you can eat midmorning and midafternoon as part of your good nutrition program.

Overall, a rainbow diet of multicolored vegetables and fruits, grains and sources of protein, with various textures is not only healthier, but also more enjoyable to look at and consume. So, before you take a bite of your food, look at the food arranged on your plate. Make sure there is a variety of colors represented and take a moment to appreciate the visual aspects of the food. Smell the food before you eat it as a means of further appreciation. Make a statement of gratitude before eating; gratitude for the farmers, suppliers, cooks, as well as for the food itself.

The body needs more than 50 different nutrients, like vitamins, each day. To get them, you need to eat a variety of foods. The main food groups are: grains and legumes, vegetables and fruits, dairy and meat products and alternatives. Please note that sugar and caffeine are NOT food groups!

A balanced diet needs to include all these different nutrients:

- **Complex Carbohydrates** are needed for energy
- **Protein** is needed so that the body can build and repair
- **Healthy Fats** also provide energy and they are required for some essential chemical reactions
- **Vitamins** are needed by the body in order to perform essential metabolic activities
- **Minerals** are necessary for metabolism and to keep the body functioning
- **Water** is essential as it accounts for 70% of the composition of the body. It provides a medium for chemical reactions.

If we fail to get enough of these nutrients the body will suffer.

Alcohol use is one of the major causes of nutritional deficiency. Some vitamins important for mental health include iron, folate, and vitamins B6 and B12. Deficiencies of any of these nutrients can mimic mental health problems such as depression, fatigue, poor attention, and altered sleep. A lack of these nutrients causes anemia and nervous system problems. Damage to the liver and pancreas results in an imbalance of fluids, calories, protein and electrolytes. About 70 percent of people are Vitamin D deficient, and this rate is higher for substance abusers. Deficiencies may be implicated in cognitive impairment, depression, and bipolar disorder. Ask your doctor or nutritionist about vitamin and mineral supplementation, if needed.

Protein is a major player in your diet. Because it has such an important function in the body, you need a fair share of protein every single day. The primary sources of protein are common meat products like chicken, beef, pork and fish. If you're trying to reduce your daily meat intake, try some of these sources of protein and additional vital nutrients: quinoa, soy products, Greek yogurt, cottage cheese, chia seeds, chickpeas (garbanzo beans), nuts, lentils, edamame, tofu, seitan, tempeh, or peanut butter.

Dietary Fiber is also known as "roughage." It is the part of food that can't be broken down during digestion. It plays an important role in keeping your digestive system in working order and may reduce the risk of some types of cancer, heart disease, and Type 2 diabetes. Fiber comes in two forms--insoluble (whole-grain products such as wheat bran cereal, vegetables and fruit)--and soluble (peas, beans, oat bran, whole grains, barley, cereals, seeds, rice, crackers, many vegetables and fruits and some pasta, and other bakery products).

Total Fat represents the combined fats that provide energy to the body. Some types of fat are healthier than others. Saturated fat is a type of fat that is solid at room temperature. It is usually animal-based and is associated with certain health risks. Try to limit red meat to twice a week or less and avoid eating the skin on poultry. Trans fat is created when liquid fat is turned into solid fat during manufacturing. It has no food value and should be replaced with unsaturated fat whenever possible. Unsaturated fat is a type of fat that is liquid at room temperature and is typically plant based. Examples are: olive, canola, soy, corn, sunflower, peanut and nut oils. You can also get your good fats in nuts, seeds, avocados and fatty fish, notably cold-water fish like salmon, sardines and mackerel.

Carbohydrates are your body's main source of energy and aid in the production of serotonin, which facilitates a happy, stable mood. They also aid in sleep and help curb food cravings and depression. Without this macronutrient, the brain can't properly function, blood sugar becomes unstable, and neurotransmitters become disrupted. Complex carbohydrates (green vegetables, fresh fruits, beans and nuts) are better for you than simple carbohydrates (refined and processed junk food) and release energy over a longer period of time. Refined breads, candy and sugary cereal and "diet" drinks and desserts are merely a 'quick fix' and turn to fat more quickly.

Omega-3 fatty acid consumption may help with depression by assisting in the uptake of neurotransmitters and decreasing inflammation. Having a proper balance of omega-6 and omega-3 fatty acids helps neurotransmitter receptors function, which in turn helps increase the amount of neurotransmitters that can be active in the brain. Research is showing benefits for cognitive capacities across a lifespan in addition to reduction of aggression and symptoms of ADHD, and depressive disorders. The protein in fish and shellfish comes with the benefit of omega-3 fatty acids, reported to decrease the risk of coronary artery disease. Supplements containing polyunsaturated fatty acids have been recommended to help reduce anxiety in people with substance abuse.

The average American consumes about 22 teaspoons of sugar a day. Research finds that excess sugar can increase blood pressure, lower "good" HDL cholesterol levels, increase your risk of heart disease, diabetes and obesity. Keep high-sugar candy bars, cookies and other foods to a minimum. They don't contain the nutrition you need, and only give you energy for a short while. Sugary baked goods and "energy bars" can spoil your appetite for healthier meals. Instead, have an apple, some berries or a grapefruit. Their sugars are absorbed slowly.

Sugar hides in white bread, white rice and white pasta. Your best alternatives are whole grains and steel-cut oats. Also, one glass of juice has as much sugar as several pieces of fruit, but no fiber to slow absorption. Opt for eating whole fruit over drinking juice.

Keep your body hydrated for clear thinking and better performance. Drink six to eight cups of water a day. Soda, energy drinks and coffee don't count as healthy liquids. Limit your caffeine intake to no more than 3 or 4 cups (8 oz. each) a day. Decaffeinated coffee has about 3% of a regular cup of coffee, so you may want to try that as a substitute.

Possible Actions for Implementation

- Eat slowly to give the brain time to register that hunger is satisfied.
- Drink lots of liquids throughout your day (water, herbal or green tea, coconut water or green juice).
- Eat at least 5 to 9 servings of fruits and vegetables every day (fresh, canned, frozen).
- Choose whole grain bread and cereal. Eliminate cereals with added sugar.
- Use less salt, sugar and saturated fat.
- Eat more beans and grains.
- Reduce servings of red meat and processed meats, such as bacon, deli/luncheon meats, hot dogs.
- Choose low-fat milk and cheeses.
- Choose lean meats, poultry and fish.
- Stick to regular mealtimes.
- Get more protein, complex carbohydrates, and dietary fiber.
- Vitamin and mineral supplements (B-complex, zinc, and vitamins A & C) may be helpful during recovery.

Now that you know what to eat and why, let's talk about knowing what's in the food you buy and serving sizes.

Most store bought food is in a package with nutritional composition on the back of the package. Understanding what the Nutrition Facts Label includes can help you make food choices that are best for your health and recovery. Here are the basics you should know:

1. **Serving Size** - These are given in familiar measurements such as cups or pieces. This section shows how many servings are in the package, and how big the serving is. It is common for a food package to contain more than one serving, so read carefully.
2. **Calorie Count** - Calories content shows how many calories there are in one serving. A product that's fat-free, for example, isn't necessarily calorie-free. Read the label to see how many calories are in one serving of the food.
3. **Percent (%) Daily Value** - Based on a 2,000-calorie diet, this section tells you how the nutrients in one serving contribute to your total daily diet. Use it to choose foods that are high in the nutrients you should get more of, and low in the nutrients you want less of. Your nutritional needs largely depend on how physically active you are. Talk with your healthcare provider to see what calorie level is right for you

Meal planning is essential. Here are examples of healthy breakfast and snack choices:

Breakfast Ideas
- Fresh fruit, Low fat yogurt, whole wheat toast or muffin
- Fresh fruit, whole wheat bagel with peanut butter, skim milk
- Eggs as you like them, with fruit and whole wheat toast

Snack Ideas
- Fresh fruit
- Small handful of almonds
- Low-fat yogurt
- 4 crackers and a thumb-size piece of cheese
- A piece of lean meat on a piece of whole wheat bread
- Almond butter on celery

Describe what you think are healthy lunch and dinner choices and share these ideas with your group or support person:

Lunch Menu:

Dinner Menu:

Name several of your favorite snacks and one of your favorite meals?

How would you rate them in terms of nutrition?

Here is a summary of the steps to healthy eating:

1. Make good nutrition part of everyday living.
2. Eat well at home, work and play: 50% veggies and fruit, 25% whole grains, and 25% meat, poultry or fish or other sources of protein.
3. Quit the clean plate club; eat for nutrition, not out of boredom, anger or depression.
4. Don't drink your calories (sugar-laden colas, milk shakes, high-calorie sports drinks)
5. Avoid so-called "energy drinks"

Your Ideas

Name five things you can do this week to start eating better:

Make a meal plan for a whole week. Write it in the pages in Appendix A. Then make a grocery list to match your meal plan. This is to make sure you have what you need and there is not waste of food (and therefore, your money). Shop for what you need and nothing more.

Benefits of Good Nutrition

- Healthy Heart
- Bone and Teeth Strength
- Higher Energy Levels
- Brain Health
- Weight Control
- Decreased cancer risk
- Blood Sugar Control
- Anti-aging
- Immune Boosting
- Improved Mood
- Better skin tone

Unfortunately, large corporations have taken over much of our food supply in the last several decades. Our most nutritious food is to be found at Farmer's Markets and small groceries. This is not as convenient as large super markets, but it is likely worth your time and effort to shop carefully, ask questions and read labels. Supporting our organic farmers and those who raise and kill animals humanely are to be supported when possible.

CHAPTER 2
Exercise: We are Designed to Move

Aerobic Exercise is Healthful, Inexpensive and Insufficiently Utilized for a Variety of Psychiatric Disorders
—Harvard Medical Letter

The Reasons Why

Exercise is a key to mental health. Our bodies are mechanical miracles that enable us to walk, run, lift and play. As we use them, our bodies adapt and flourish. Our muscles grow stronger, our bones tougher, our hearts more powerful. Health improves as we become leaner and fitter and less likely to develop chronic diseases, such as diabetes, obesity, high blood pressure or cancer.

Exercise benefits the brain and mind. We know that the brain is amazingly responsive and can even increase in size when stimulated by exercise or meditation, or when fed a healthy diet. When we walk or work out, more blood and oxygen flow to the brain and over time, new blood vessels form and the new blood vessels become permanent. Any kind of movement is good, but, according to research, vigorous exercise for 30 minutes regularly is especially helpful.

Human beings were made to move. I'll show you how to get moving so you can enjoy your life to the fullest. Exercise offers you both preventative and therapeutic psychological benefits. While it is obvious that your feelings can influence your movement, you may not know that your movement can impact your feelings, too. For example, when you feel tired and sad, you tend to move more slowly. When you feel anxious, you may rush around or be stuck, frozen. Research shows that the connection between your brain and your body is a "two-way street," and that means that movement can change your brain, too. Exercise and recreation provide opportunities to get away from "it all" and to either enjoy some solitude or make friends and build support networks.

People beginning a program of recovery, must tend to the body first. It is likely that alcoholism or addiction has caused your body to become deconditioned and your immune system to be weakened. A well thought out, planned exercise program begins the process of rebuilding both.

Make a note here about your current level of fitness. What kind of shape is your body in?

_____

_____

_____

_____

_____

_____

The mental benefits of exercise have a neurochemical basis. Movement reduces levels of the body's stress hormones, such as adrenaline and cortisol. It also stimulates the production of endorphins, chemicals in the brain that are the body's natural painkillers and mood elevators. When you exercise, your body boosts critical brain chemicals—dopamine, noradrenaline, and serotonin--which create a natural high. When you exercise, chemicals that your brain associates with rewarding behaviors are released, giving you feelings of wellbeing and relaxation that you may have only gotten in the past through substance abuse.

However, abuse of drugs and alcohol causes an imbalance that eventually interferes with your ability to feel pleasure, happiness, and satisfaction. Dedicated physical activity helps you reintroduce natural levels of endorphins into your system. This not only helps you feel better, but also re-teaches your body that it is capable of regulating its own brain chemistry and mood in healthy, natural ways.

Have you noticed the feelings of relaxation and optimism that accompany a hard workout—or the hot shower after your exercise is over? This is due to a release of endorphins, the "feel-good" hormones. Regular exercise makes your brain's "fight or flight" system less reactive, and keeps you calmer longer. Elite athletes say exercise keeps their moods stable. And, they are not the only ones! It appears true that regular aerobic exercise, in many cases, may be just as effective as antidepressants. It's also cheaper, with fewer side effects.

In addition to the chemical changes happening in your brain when you exercise, working out can reduce the negative effects of giving up your substance(s) or behavior(s), which include sleep troubles, anxiety, depression, and weight gain. Simply by improving your overall health and well-being, regular exercise rebuilds your body and your immune system, and gives you a healthy way to release difficult or pent-up emotions, including anger, sadness and frustration.

When you are anxious or fearful, you may experience rapid heartbeat and have trouble focusing and concentrating. Exercise can focus your thoughts, increase your energy, and reduce feelings of confusion fatigue and depression. In the Meditation section of this workbook, you learn how the meditative movement of Qigong, tai chi, or yoga can reduce stress as well as provide exercise for the body. Changing your posture, breathing, and rhythm can change your brain, reducing stress, depression and anxiety and leading to general feelings of wellbeing.

Through movement, you can refocus your thoughts on your wellbeing and forget, at least briefly, all of whatever else is going on in your life. You may leave your workout with a clearer mind, feeling more rejuvenated and optimistic. Finding this clarity within chaos can make recovery more sustainable.

You don't need to be a fitness fanatic or marathoner to reap the benefits of exercise, but you do need to develop a routine. Making fitness part of everyday can help stave off cravings, reduce stress and avoid major illnesses.

You can exercise by yourself or with others. Meet a friend in the morning for a walk or sign up for a class at the Y or a local gym. Exercising with someone else can boost how you feel about yourself and relationships. When you synchronize your movement with others, studies indicate that you like them more and feel more charitable toward them. That's probably why dance therapy can help depression and anxiety. Your mind and body are intimately connected. While your brain is the master control system for your body's movement, the way you move can also affect the way you think and feel. Having a regularly scheduled time to devote to exercise can help when you need to destress or retreat to have time for yourself.

When you are too exhausted to use thought control strategies such as focusing on the positive, or looking at a troubling situation from a different perspective, movement can come to the rescue. By working out, going on a meditative walk by yourself, or going for a walk with someone, you can feel better.

Nothing is quick and easy, but with the right attitude and goals in mind, you will enjoy the journey you are undertaking. It has worked for countless others, and it can work for you. If you are not as strong as you'd like to be, understand that the physical benefits come with time, but the mental and emotional perks of exercise happen right away. So, make it happen for you!

Possible Actions for Implementation

YOU are all you need to start and continue a successful exercise program. You don't need to invest in an expensive health club membership or have the latest athletic wear or high-tech equipment. If you have floor space, try simple floor exercises. You can get in shape with many different types of training or activity and YouTube is filled with exercise routines if you don't know where to begin. Type in "Exercise for Beginners," and a menu of possibilities will pop up.

Many cities have free classes, maps of walking trails and bird-watching sites, fitness parks and bike trails. Local high schools or colleges offer swim passes for their pools and access to tennis and running tracks. There are televised fitness shows, downloadable exercise regimens, and so much more.

You may want to hire a personal trainer or experienced buddy who can help you stay motivated and challenged during the early weeks of training. You'll want to do things correctly to prevent injury and discouragement. Be sure that your exercise program is appropriately varied to include strength training, aerobics, flexibility and core training. Typically you will need to move your body fast enough to get your heart rate to maximum number of beats per minute (220 minus your age). No matter what your current fitness level, committing to a regular exercise program, and getting some type of physical activity most days of the week, is an incredibly effective way to support maintaining your recovery.

The most important thing is that you like what you're doing and that you are willing to be a little adventurous. Try not to focus on perfection or what others can do. Focus instead on increasing your healthy behavior. Make it a habit to walk 15 minutes a day, and add time, distance, and intensity from there. Remember, everyone starts somewhere. So, if you are already a devoted exerciser, keep it up. If you are new to a regular exercise regimen, just get started. And, if you encounter your own resistance, please know that this is common. We are creatures of habit and getting a new habit in place can be challenging. But, it is doable, so don't give up!

Before getting started, let's talk about your resistance, if you have some. Please write down the reasons you think you can't add exercise to your daily life.

_____

_____

_____

_____

Now write about what you might do to overcome your resistance. By the way, resistance is normal. Our ancestors, whose DNA we have, tried to avoid expending energy. So much energy was involved in survival that they did not have to plan exercise; it was automatic and essential. Often, that resistance and avoidance is built into our DNA.

_____

_____

_____

_____

_____

Think of the ways you can add exercise to your daily routine. You can participate in brisk walking, playing a sport, doing yoga or working out in the gym. You can combine these activities into a routine that changes from day to day, if you like. You need to exercise at least three times a week for 30 minutes at a time to provide valuable physical improvement. If you want to experience cognitive benefits, you'll need to combine strength training with aerobics to achieve more strenuous exercise.

You will begin to see benefits within a month of regular physical activity, and will likely notice that your mood is better and more stable and you are more energetic. Importantly, you'll also have the satisfaction of knowing you're doing something for yourself and your wellbeing. These benefits increase over the course of six months.

Write down some ideas you have to add a regular exercise routine to your week. If you already have a routine, write down what you do and where you see there could be improvement.

_____

_____

_____

_____

_____

_____

It goes without saying that you should speak with your health care advisor before beginning any sort of exercise program. When you have the OK, I have described some ideas about how to begin.

Except during illness, you should exercise nearly every day to stay healthy and reduce stress. That doesn't necessarily mean training for a marathon or swimming laps, but it does mean:
- 30 to 40 minutes of moderate exercise such as walking or 15 to 20 minutes of vigorous exercise.
- Walk at least two miles a day, or do the equivalent amount of another activity. You can do it all at once or in 10- to 15-minute chunks if that fits your schedule better.
- Add a little strength training and stretching two to three times a week
- If you need more help with stress, consider deep breathing or muscle relaxation exercises.

Any type of physical activity can be transformed into an exercise routine and before long, all the fun you have translates into tremendous health benefits.

WAYS TO GET A WORKOUT

- Walking for fitness
- Running/Jogging
- Treadmill
- Aerobics Classes
- Stairmaster
- Rowing
- Yoga
- Tennis
- Racquet ball
- Marathons or Triathlons
- Pilates
- Kick boxing
- Free Weights, Hand Weights
- Bicycling
- Tai Chi
- Weight/resistance machines
- Weight Training
- Stretching
- Swimming
- Standup Paddling
- Shuffleboard
- Bocce Ball

Hiking/Walking – A simple 30-minute walk outdoors can stave off cravings as well as boost overall brain function by supporting new brain cell growth.

Strength Training – Weight training or bodyweight exercises like push-ups can help reboot the body's sleep cycle and relieve insomnia.

Team Sports – Why not double lifetime benefits derived from working out with others? Throwing the ball, shooting some hoops, or cycling with other people will provide more than a good workout. The social interaction with friends or like-minded people will help you replace old, unhealthy activities with new healthy ones. Exercising outdoors in the company of others allows you to "check the boxes" on three of the *8 Ways to Wellbeing*. It's not about having to train hard or train long. It's more about just getting out there and moving.

Obstacle Courses, rock climbing walls and rope courses are physical challenges that can boost your self-confidence as dopamine is released in your brain. The memories made during these exercises can be strong reminders that you're capable of overcoming any hurdle.

Set realistic goals and timelines. All significant life changes take patience and commitment in practicing the new principles and skills. Use your support system to surround yourself with exercise buddies, coaches or workout buddies to help you stick to your plan. Stop comparing yourself to other people in fantastic shape and focus on your own efforts, endurance and changes. Recognize your accomplishments, beginning with just getting up and moving. It all counts.

Behavioral factors contribute to the emotional benefits to you. As your waistline shrinks and your strength and stamina increase, your self-image will improve. You'll earn a sense of mastery and control, of pride and self-confidence. Your renewed vigor and energy will help you succeed in many tasks, and the discipline of regular exercise will help you achieve your lifestyle goals. Enjoy feelings of accomplishment, pride and self worth as you reach benchmarks in your long-term goals. Denial and delay are enemies of the new you. Get started today, with just a walk around the block. Eliminate the usual excuses: no time, not the right shoes, no exercise clothes, too tired, no one to exercise with…etc. If you hate the gym, try dancing, tennis, walking, home programs, or gardening instead. **Realize that exercise is part of relapse prevention.**

There is another benefit that is not talked about much, but that is important, and that is that long-term muscle tension leads to what is called muscle armor tension patterns. The body becomes habituated to being in a tense posture, which is unhealthy. Flexibility is lost and the rigidity of the muscles leads to chronic pain. Regular exercise, as well as deep tissue massage may help release this muscle armor and create more flexibility and reduce chronic pain.

As with anything new you learn, the more you do it, the better you get. If you have been inactive for a while, start with a simple walking program, and gradually increase the frequency or length of your walks as you feel stronger. Add more intensity to your regimen and you'll realize the physical and mental health benefits and feel more competent in your ability to meet the challenges you will face in recovery. Following these guidelines and consistently applying the knowledge you've gained will give you life-long satisfaction.

Your Ideas

This week, schedule 30-minutes of physical movement for at least 3 days and add more days if you can.

Day, Date, Time	Exercise
Day 1	
Day 2	
Day 3	
Day 4	
Day 5	
Day 6	
Day 7	

Now make some notes about what worked and what didn't work. What, if anything, needs new planning to make this sustainable?

_____

_____

_____

_____

_____

_____

Now, see what you can do to keep your momentum. Use the charts in Appendix A to keep track of your exercise. Remember that the research says that people who chart their progress, using check marks, gold stars, or whatever little "reward" they like, actually do better at sustaining whatever habit they are trying to integrate into their routine.

Benefits of Regular Exercise

- Improves mood and sense of well-being
- Adds structure, which makes life more manageable so recovery is more sustainable
- Increases energy, improves sleep and overall health
- Improves cognitive function to find clarity within chaos
- Prevents and heals disorders such as addiction, anxiety and depression
- Improves immune function
- Improves cholesterol
- Reduces blood sugar
- Reduces the risk of heart attack, stroke, colon and breast cancers, osteoporosis and fractures
- Reduces chronic pain
- Reduces age-related memory loss and the severity of Alzheimer's and Parkinson's diseases
- Improves flexibility, balance and agility
- Releases endorphins for pleasurable feelings
- Enhances self-efficacy and self esteem
- Interrupts negative thoughts
- Releases chronic psychosomatic muscle tension
- Become leaner and fitter
- Aids in sweating toxins out of the body
- Improves muscle strength
- Improves circulation
- Sharpens mental skills including executive function
- Improves body image and toning
- Improves flow of oxygen, breathing

Exercise is something that most everyone can do in some form. You don't have to be an elite athlete to take a walk in your neighborhood in the morning and evening. The natural anti-anxiety and mood elevation properties of exercise may take awhile to be noticeable. So, keep at it. Make exercise a daily enterprise. You'll be glad you did.

CHAPTER 3

Relaxation: Breathe In, Breathe Out...Aaah

"Mindfulness is the single most powerful tool available for those seeking freedom from addiction."
—Tara Brach, Ph.D., author of *Radical Acceptance*

The Reasons Why

Practicing relaxation through mindfulness, stillness, silence and attention will change your life. The benefits of relaxation are endless in our world that values over-stimulation, and where we see more people, often travel further daily, and encounter sensory over-stimulation of every sort more frequently than our ancestors did in a lifetime. Though we humans were really not made for this sort of speed and the constant decision-making and pressure that it requires, it has now become the norm. There really is no way I know of to avoid it altogether outside of entering a monastery or other means of withdrawing from the world. We all need ways to quiet the mind and relax the body.

According to Dr. Walsh's research, we need a time of quiet, a time with few, if any distractions, a time for just being in the present moment. This is the essence of what is often called *mindfulness meditation.* The healing and soothing practice of spending deliberate time quieting the mind, reducing sensory stimuli, and practicing mindfulness will give you peace and serenity. Welcome this quiet, as well as mindful awareness, for both rest and insight. In addition, it was the famed German psychiatrist, Victor Frankl who said, "Between stimulus and response, there is a space. In that space is our power to choose our response.

In our response lies our growth and freedom." Often, recovering people need more time between a stimulus, such as, "I want to get high," and a response, such as, "I think I'll call a recovery friend instead." Learning mindfulness is a good way to begin to have that pause that Dr. Frankl was referring to.

In this chapter, you will learn suggested ways of coping with the demands of a busy life, as well as techniques to prevent relapse in recovery through relaxation and mindfulness. These practices will help you to:
1. Realize the potential of self-direction (as opposed to "going along to get along")
2. Assume personal responsibility as a major factor in health and sickness
3. Minimize detrimental effects of stress and distress
4. Achieve and maintain a high level of feelings of wellbeing
5. Improve impulse control, so vital to recovering people

The stress of everyday life and the work of maintaining your recovery can undermine your wellbeing on many levels. Even though stress is universal, few people are trained in managing it. Therefore, many people respond self-destructively— aided by the ever-present unhealthy influence of advertising, celebrity "role models," and availability of drugs and alcohol— to cope with pressure and temptation. Temporary fixes are just that, temporary, often leaving you feeling worse or causing more problems. So, learning tools for stress management is essential to living your life plan and achieving both short-term and long-term goals.

I have identified four forms of stress: 1) behavioral stress comes when we are physically challenged or exhausted, 2) emotional stress comes when our feelings have been hurt or upset in some way, 3) intellectual stress happens when we have been stretching our capacity for learning new material, and 4) psychological stress occurs when our values or beliefs are challenged. Stress can be either acute or chronic. Acute stress is a response to a current significant challenge. Chronic stress by comparison, is ongoing and produces a constant state of anxious arousal. By learning mindfulness meditation techniques, as well as other methods for improved coping, you can use stress constructively to promote good health and self-development.

It is a fact that people who are susceptible to addiction and relapse from addiction tend to be stress sensitive, meaning that they are especially sensitive to one or more of the types of stress previously identified. When you have learned new ways of coping with stressful situations, your sense of self-efficacy will be strengthened and the probability of relapse will be decreased. One of the most potent and readily accessible coping mechanisms we have at our disposal is mindfulness meditation.

G. Alan Marlatt, Ph.D. wrote, "One of the most significant effects of regular meditation practice is the development of mindfulness: the capacity to observe the ongoing process of experience without at the same time becoming 'attached' or identifying with the content of each thought, feeling, or image. Mindfulness is a particularly effective cognitive skill in relapse prevention. If clients can acquire this ability through the regular practice of meditation, they may be able to 'detach' themselves from the lure of urges, cravings, or cognitive rationalizations that may otherwise lead to a lapse."

We all have urges and cravings and our rationale for indulging ourselves in these. So, Dr. Marlatt is saying that in order to avoid giving in to the urges and cravings that are a part of recovery, we need a means of counter-acting them that enhances recovery and our overall functioning. He says that in his experience, Mindfulness Meditation is just such a means and a tool.

Please note in the space provided some of the stresses that stimulate urges and cravings in you.

_____

_____

_____

_____

_____

It's important to note that stress is the product of an entire lifestyle, not just the product of an occasional crisis, death of a loved one, argument, disturbing news, high-stimulus situations or road rage. Consequently, monitoring your internal arousal level is important; meaning, how anxious do you feel at any given time or in general? Stress management is a personal skill, because *coping* cannot be delegated to someone else; it must be internalized as a part of your personal makeup.

Have you had experience with Relaxation through Mindfulness or Meditation? Please write about your experience and your willingness to participate in this form of Relaxation at this time.

_____

_____

_____

_____

_____

_____

Identifying your stress signals to prevent tensions from building up and ultimately losing control over your choices and behavior is important. You can learn to reduce your tensions before they are anything more than a clenched jaw or a quickened pulse. You can be that relaxed person whose honesty, ability to reflect and self-acceptance keeps you in charge of yourself.

For some, stress is no more than anxiety or physical nervousness, but for others, stress can lead to despair and mental illness. Making a conscious effort to be aware of the physical signs that mean your body is anticipating "fight, flight or freeze" is an important part of stress reduction. We get physical hints of what is to come before it happens, if we can just catch the signs early. Some possible early warning signals might be:

- Stepped-up breathing
- Sweaty palms
- Butterflies in the stomach
- Racing heart
- Perspiration
- Muscular tension
- Feelings of unhappiness and/or depression
- An overabundance of nervous energy.

Chapter 3 | Relaxation: Breathe In, Breathe Out...Aaah

What happens for you when you are overly stressed?

_____

_____

_____

_____

_____

_____

What do you usually do to relax and distress?

_____

_____

_____

_____

_____

_____

Recovering people often experience considerable guilt and shame about their past behavior while abusing drugs or alcohol. These are challenging emotions to cope with and can, in and of themselves lead to relapse. For that reason, its important to keep your eye on the present moment and have a means of transforming these thoughts into actions that shift the energy from negative to positive. Therefore, establishing a mindfulness practice, which keeps you in the present moment, as well as other relaxation techniques, is essential to long-term recovery.

John Kabat-Zinn defined mindfulness, saying, "Mindfulness is a way of paying attention on purpose, in the present moment, and nonjudgmentally." When we can see and experience things as they are in the present moment, instead of dwelling endlessly on the regrets of the past, or our anxiety and worry about the future and where the next *fix* is coming from, we begin to have agency for directing our lives in meaningful and thoughtful ways." In addition, recovery emphasizes acknowledging, feeling and experiencing upsets and discomfort when they arise, and not trying to escape these feelings, but rather, learning to tolerate them as the passing and mostly temporary experiences we all have. Its likely that you have heard the maxim, "Pause when agitated," in 12 Step meetings, and its good advice. Mindfulness emphasizes that those circumstances, whether physical, environmental, emotional or psychological, are changing all the time, and as *The Bible* says, "This, too, shall pass."

Though I am emphasizing a mindfulness meditation practice, I know that you probably have some healthy ways you have discovered in which you "kick back and relax." In the space below, write some examples of healthy ways in which you typically relax.

_____

_____

_____

_____

_____

Possible Actions for Implementation

If you have trouble thinking about what to do to unwind, here are some suggestions:
- Go for a walk
- Take some time out and focus on what's happening around you
- Listen to quiet and relaxing music
- Go fishing
- Take a bath
- Go to a movie or watch a DVD
- Focus your attention on a puzzle
- Read a book
- Do yoga
- Repeat affirmations

- Breathe in counting to 4; hold for 4; and exhale for count of 4.
- Take time to develop or continue a hobby
- Color in an adult coloring book

I recommend formal Mindfulness Meditation as a daily practice for relaxation and optimizing mental health. Ask your therapist or other knowledgeable person to help you find a teacher and stay with the teacher until you have established your own sustainable practice.

Start by setting aside 10 minutes a day to sit quietly with eyes closed or lowered as a start. Place your feet on the floor and hands, with palms up and open on your lap. Get comfortable. Choose a word or brief prayer or affirmation to repeat silently. Or, you can count your breaths, breathing slowly and deeply, so that you can feel the rise and fall of your belly. Set a quiet timer ahead of time so that you don't have to worry about when to end. Typically, your mind will wander. No judging … just gently bring your mind back to the word(s) you have chosen, or silence. You may be surprised at how difficult this is if you are a beginner. But, in time, you will begin to look forward to this quiet recharging of your energy.

When you have done this three times on three different days, write your experience (easy/hard, boring/interesting, relaxing/tense, etc.).

_____

_____

_____

_____

_____

_____

It can be helpful to begin your mindfulness practice by using a CD or smart phone App to get you started. There are seemingly endless CDs and Apps available and I have made a partial list in the Resources section. I suggest you try out several of them and see what you like. But, like anything else, it only works if you do it consistently.

There has been much written about Mindfulness Meditation for Relaxation and this is a chapter that could be a book in itself. But, for our purposes here, the idea is to set aside a time each day for Mindfulness Meditation for Relaxation. The goal is to begin with 5-10 minutes of silence, where you are focused on your breathing and using the word or phrase that you have chosen to help you stay present to your breathing. Hopefully this will extend to 20, 30 or more minutes each day over time. You will be pleased with the results and rewarded with the benefits I have suggested.

Your Ideas

What is the best time in your regular day to set aside for Mindfulness Meditation practice?

_____

_____

Who or what will help you to maintain this practice until it can become a habit?

_____

_____

The key principle of a more relaxed approach to life is balance, arranging your life in such a way that your needs are fulfilled in healthy proportion and you don't become overloaded with any of the experiences or events that produce intolerable stress and lead to relapse.

This workbook takes a synergistic approach to healing and wellness. That is, the combined action of the eight areas of wellness produce a balance of many dimensions of living and working in order to achieve a quality of life which is productive, nurturing and satisfying. What you do in one area, supports, enhances, and capitalizes on actions in the others. Conversely, if one or more aspects of your life are unattended to or awry, your equilibrium is thrown off balance, often with unfavorable results. Wellness is an attainable goal for you. It takes practice, but the rewards are worth it.

As a final note, one important way to reduce stress is something indigenous people call "shape shifting." Shape shifting means shifting the energy or your point of view about the challenging situation. For example, if something or someone is bothering or upsetting you, say to yourself, "There is another way to see this (person/situation)." Then, ask yourself, "What is another way to see this person or situation?" When you are able to change your view or perception of the situation, you have shape-shifted it. I am not talking about denying what is so, but rather, changing your point of view to one that is more positive and useful.

Chapter 3 | Relaxation: Breathe In, Breathe Out...Aaah

Just as a slight shift in the tilt of a kaleidoscope changes the whole design you see, a small change in your point of view of a person or situation will provide you with relief and a less stressful way of seeing it. This is a powerful stress reduction technique.

Describe a situation that you would like to shape shift.

_____
_____
_____
_____
_____
_____

Now describe another way you could see this that would not be false but would shift the energy to something more positive and less stressful.

_____
_____
_____
_____
_____
_____
_____

Your stress response is individual to your life experiences, mental and physical state. Responses can span a spectrum from regression and disability, to resilience and normal functioning, to growth and strength. Three basic coping techniques are:

1. Managing the number of stressors you encounter by controlling the pace of your life.
2. Fortifying your stress filter through physical and mental conditioning to reduce the harmful effects of stressful events.
3. Directing your stress responses into positive attitudes and behaviors (shape-shifting) and personal effectiveness.

What causes you the most noticeable stress? List the top 10 triggers that make you uncomfortable, reduce your functioning, and/or cause you to be tempted to relapse or behave badly. They can be people, situations, times, places, events, moments, goings or comings. Take your time to think of times you lost control and acted out.

My Top 10 Triggers (Write down Who, What, Why, Where, When, and How You Acted)

1.

2.

3.

4.

5.

6.

7.

8. _____

9. _____

10. _____

Using Mindfulness Meditation and other relaxation techniques for stress management is important for mental health. Stress can make your body adapt and become stronger, and it can even be good when it pushes you to learn new skills, stretch your limits, or encourage you to reach new levels of mastery and success; in short, to thrive. Make the distinction between *distress* and *eustress*. Distress causes you to feel upset or overwhelmed. Eustress is the excitement and pressure that comes from competition that you choose to engage in, for example. It's the positive reaction to the stress that generates within you a desire to achieve and overcome a challenge. So, it is your perceptions of a stressor, to some degree, that determine if you are feeling distress or eustress.

When it is severe or chronic, unrelieved stress can exact a toll on both body and mind. Mentally, it can become anxiety and depression. Physically, it can cause adrenal failure or other medical crises.

This is where your Mindfulness Meditation for Relaxation practice comes into play. Having a daily practice is like putting money in a savings account for unexpected expenses. When unexpected stresses occur, you will have enough resources in the "bank" to manage the situation without being triggered into relapse.

There are many ways you can keep stress under control in your life. As you are learning in this workbook, exercise, health-enhancing recreation, good nutrition, positive relationships and spiritual practice can benefit you.

Movement is a great stress management strategy when it is rhythmic in nature and performed slowly. Walking meditation, tai chi, qi gong, reading for pleasure and other TLCs can be relaxing. Yoga offers both somatic (body) and contemplative (mind) strategies. Along with meditation, it has been shown to enhance various psychological capacities, health, and maturity. Focused meditation is one of the most direct ways to activate and strengthen those areas in the brain that increase empathy, which is one reason that I emphasize it in this chapter.

Muscle relaxation therapies which require you to systematically tighten and then relax major muscle groups can be beneficial for you, particularly in treating panic and generalized anxiety. Try muscle contractions before bed. Before you fall asleep at night, take turns tensing each muscle group – squeezing it – and then relaxing it. Start all the way at your toes and work up your body to the crown of your head.

Coloring books and puzzles with tranquil scenes or elegant patterns are popular ways to slow down. Practice deep breathing; throughout the day, take a moment to take a couple of deep breaths. Breathe in through the nose for a count of four and out through the nose for a count of eight.

Try deep breathing for two minutes right now and note your experience.

Remember that relaxation, physical rest, meditation, and mindfulness are all interconnected. The more you practice, the better you will get. It takes a while to establish the practice, so don't get discouraged. Stick with it. You will become good at it and your quality of life will leap forward.

Benefits of Relaxation

- Slows your heart rate
- Lowers blood pressure
- Slows your breathing rate
- Reduces activity of stress hormones
- Increases blood flow to major muscles
- Reduces muscle tension and chronic pain
- Reduces depression
- Reduces anxiety
- Improves concentration and mood
- Improves sleep
- Manages chronic headaches and other types of chronic pain
- Lowers fatigue

In the chart below, log your date and time of practicing Mindfulness Meditation or other techniques for relaxation.

Date	Time Spent	Practice Technique

CHAPTER 4

Recreation

"Sometimes the inessential is essential!"
— T. L Reese

The Reasons Why

Recreation, humor and play not only feel good, but also do us good. Playfulness is built into our biology, as we can see in most species—puppies, kittens, monkeys and children. Children's play is more than having fun. It is a way of experimenting, expanding limits, training muscles, and developing minds. Play is a way of learning to live together, learning how to compete and cooperate, to make friends and acquire social skills. It's fun, but also an integral part of learning and growing. It's the same for adults and it is a critical aspect of a healthy lifestyle.

Leisure is your discretionary time spent in non-compulsory activities, time spent away from obligations, cares and work. Because leisure time is free from compulsory activities such as employment, running a business, childcare, household chores, school and other such day-to-day activities, not including eating, and sleeping, it is often referred to as "free time." For adults, "down time" is beneficial as we recreate, refresh and revitalize ourselves. We speed up our recovery from the stresses of work, reduce painful emotions and foster feelings of happiness and joy. It is a fact that laughter is good medicine!

Involvement in enjoyable activities is central to your healthy lifestyle, and hopefully brings feelings of freedom and joy. Through experiences of positive emotions we transform ourselves, becoming more creative, knowledgeable, resilient, socially integrated, and healthy individuals. Research indicates that recreation, often synonymous with play, is something that is hardwired in our biology. You just have to find a way to do it in a way that you enjoy, but does not interfere with or jeopardize your hard-won sobriety.

How to have fun and enjoy free time in sobriety is often a big challenge and a question mark for recovering people. So many leisure activities that people in recovery have enjoyed in the past have been paired with their drug(s) of choice, that to engage in those same activities without drinking alcohol or using drugs seems odd or boring at best, and a trigger for relapse at worst. "Going drinking," may have been considered to be an activity in and of itself … and, it might have been fun, until it became destructive and dangerous.

There is something called state-dependent learning, which is a phenomenon in which memory retrieval is most efficient when the person is in the same state of consciousness as they were when the memory was formed. For example, this means that if you have only ever danced while drunk or high, you might not remember how to do it very well in your sober state. You may have to start over to learn to dance and suffer the awkwardness of being a beginner again. Likewise, if you enjoy music and going to concerts, you may find that going to the same concerts that you attended pre-recovery is not as enjoyable as you had remembered. This means that things that you found fun, entertaining or easy in the past, may not be so now.

This may not be universally true for all recovering people engaging in activities that previously gave them pleasure, but it is true often enough to come to the attention of therapists and sponsors working with them. Even something as pleasurable as sexual activity may have to be relearned in your sober state. So, please don't be alarmed about not quite knowing what to do for fun and pleasure. This is a common problem for recovering people and I hope my suggestions in this regard prove helpful to you.

Recreation includes any activities that you find enjoyable, that help you have fun and be adventurous, that challenge you and give you a needed break from everyday responsibilities. It is time out from taking care of the necessities of life and having some free time for personally gratifying pursuits.

Recreation in sobriety may require you to try some new activities that you might not have considered in the past. Not only is this a good idea from the standpoint of expanding your repertoire of possible ways to spend free time, but it is also important from the standpoint of letting go of activities that you have typically done while drinking or using.

What are some of the activities in which you engaged in the past that you associate with drinking or using?

_____
_____
_____
_____
_____
_____
_____

Have you noticed any activities that you engaged in pre-recovery that now feel awkward or uninteresting to you? Please describe.

_____
_____
_____
_____
_____
_____

Has this caused any problems for you? If so, what sort of problems?

_____
_____
_____
_____
_____
_____
_____

Are any of these activities that used to be fun, but are now challenging because you aren't as good at them now or don't find them as pleasurable worth doing with some relearning while sober?

_____
_____
_____
_____
_____

Either way, please explain.

_____
_____
_____
_____
_____

Give some examples of what makes you laugh.

_____
_____
_____
_____
_____
_____

What do you do that makes other people laugh?

Possible Actions for Implementation

The world is an enormous place with a zillion things, activities, people, places, etc. to be interested in and take pleasure in. So, just know that when you have free time and don't really know what to do with yourself, it is time for exploration. The following possibilities are just a few of an endless list of things that might interest you and give you the recreation (literally re-creation), fun, and time out that is essential to good mental health and recovery.

If you see something on this list that is a possible interest or activity, circle it for future exploration. Be aware that some activities may be more interesting depending on whether you are male or female, single or partnered, introvert or extrovert.

1. Team sports – There are leagues for bowling, indoor and outdoor soccer, softball, baseball, hockey, swimming and just about every other team sport there is. Investigate and sign up.

2. Individual sports – Archery, yoga, karate, swimming, skiing, skating, kayaking, paddle boarding, surfing, jiu jitsu, other martial arts and other individual sports.

3. Reading – The library is full of books and videos on every subject and for every taste imaginable. Ask the librarian to help you choose something you will enjoy, or sign up to join a book club.

4. Hobbies and crafts – Visit a hobby shop and choose a model to build, a sewing or knitting class to sign up for, a kit of some sort to assemble or other activity that you find of interest. Be adventurous. Try something new!

5. Take classes at your local YMCA or YWCA. Daycare is often provided at Y's, allowing those of you with children to have some time for yourself.

6. Take a class, either online or in person at your local community college or other school or studio. Have you wanted to learn to dance, cook, speak a foreign language, learn art history, and take better photos? Grab the catalog from available local resources and sign up.

7. Visit zoos, aquariums, local historical places, museums, parks, and the beach, take a walking tour of your town or a city near you.

8. Learn about the natural world by studying up on bees and beekeeping, birds and bird or birdcall identification, gardening, and volunteering at your local wildlife rehabilitation center or environmental protection/education center.

9. Find a series of podcasts that interest you. There are podcasts on every conceivable topic … finances, music, government, religion, cooking, technology, stories that are pure entertainment, etc.

10. Invite friends over for a meal or if that seems too much, just for dessert and coffee or tea. You could have people over for potluck dinner where everyone brings something. Teach them a board or card game after the meal. Make this a regular practice. Have Poker night.

11. Learn a card or other game: Bridge, Canasta, Cribbage, Go, Chess, and teach friends to play with you. Have a game night with friends.

12. Have your own film festival. Line up a series of movies or a TV series and watch them on your own, or invite friends to join you. Make popcorn and serve root beer.

13. Go camping. There are often "Friends of Bill" signs at campgrounds so that you can take in a 12 Step meeting while you enjoy the outdoors. Learn to fish.

14. Take art or ceramics lessons.

15. Take music lessons and practice in your free time.

16. Choose a college or professional sports team to follow. Learn the players by name and what is involved in playing their position.

17. Take some singing lessons and then join a choir or other singing group. Do Karaoke.

18. Write letters, cards or thank you notes (remember handwritten notes?) to friends, relatives, and the children of friends. Put their birthdays on your calendar and send them a greeting.

19. Check out the Meetup App and the activities on it for fun things to do in your area with important strangers (that's what you call friends you haven't met yet).

20. Join a little theatre group near you. Act, do lighting, pass out programs, sew costumes, etc.

21. Finally, start a savings plan for a sober vacation. Get the brochures, choose a vacation and make the budget plan to make it happen. Save that spare change and spend time rolling it in coin wrappers and getting it into your savings account that is earmarked for this vacation.

Your Ideas

Now it's your turn! List five things that you like to do for fun that are possibilities for your free time.

1. _____

2. _____

3. _____

4. _____

5. _____

Pick one that you can do really soon...like this week! _____

Now, after you have done it, write your experience. What was it like doing this activity? Is it something you'll do again?

_____

_____

_____

_____

_____

It's important that you have things to do in your free time that are fun and give you pleasure. If you do things that you notice trigger your craving, be sure to note this and speak with your sponsor or a sober friend about the experience right away. It may be best to avoid that activity for a time until you have more recovery. It is also possible that the activity that triggers your craving is just something to let go of permanently.

This brings us to the topic of renunciation. Big word! The definition of renunciation is to abandon or sacrifice something. Most often we renounce something in order to get something we consider to be better. For example, diabetics (hopefully) renounce simple sugar, etc. You may have to renounce certain activities and maybe even the people associated with them in order to have your sobriety, which is priceless. This is an important topic, because there will definitely be times that former friends, and even family, may encourage you to participate in something "fun," when you know that, for you, it will lead you into dangerous or even deadly territory.

I know a man, for example, who loves horses and loves horse racing. The problem is that he loved gambling, too, and he bet on the horse races regularly. His gambling became an addiction and he had enormous pain as a result. After going to inpatient treatment, he told me that he could no longer drink alcohol, though he wasn't a problem drinker. He couldn't go to the horse races, or watch or listen to them for obvious reasons. But, why not be able to have the occasional beer or cocktail? The reason was that the beer or other alcohol containing drink caused him to crave gambling. If he had a beer, he was more likely to call his bookie. He rightly decided that it really wasn't in his best interests to have the occasional drink. It was just too risky. He renounced gambling and the drinking that served as a trigger for the gambling in order to have what he valued more … his family, his sobriety, his job, etc. … in short, a life he could embrace.

Sometimes one seemingly harmless activity leads to a definite harmful activity. Be aware of this chain reaction and note it. And, remember, your sobriety is the best guarantee that your life will be joyful, so don't compromise it for anyone or anything!

List any activities that you know of that trigger your craving.

_____
_____
_____
_____
_____
_____
_____

List any friends or family that you are aware of who think its fun to encourage you to drink or use or engage in activities that are risky for you.

_____
_____
_____
_____
_____
_____
_____

You may think it is odd to be talking about this in a chapter on Recreation, but it is often during leisure time activities that you are social and are faced with important decisions regarding activities that are helpful to your recovery and friends who are a positive or negative influence.

This is also where the topic of assertiveness comes in because it requires that you be assertive to avoid people and activities that jeopardize your recovery, and maintain good boundaries.

Write about your ability or lack thereof to assert yourself regarding leisure activities that could trigger craving. How able are you to say "no?"

Talk with your sponsor, therapist or group members about how to manage situations where someone or something triggers a craving in you. Make any notes about the conversation here or your ideas about managing this sort of situation.

Please notice that I did not include engaging in social media, video games or other "screen" activities in this chapter on Recreation. It is not that there is anything intrinsically wrong with these activities, but they tend to be solitary pursuits. My goal is that you have interests and activities that stretch you and help you to have more variety in your leisure time activities. So, if you engage in "screen" activities, watch it! It can be addicting (the research says so), and can increase feelings of anxiety, depression and loneliness, rather than alleviate them.

Do you spend too much time looking at "screens" during leisure? Comment.

One other Recreation topic that I briefly mentioned, but have not addressed is sexual pleasure. The reason I haven't addressed sex in this section or in this workbook is that, while I am certainly sex positive, it seems just too big a topic for the purposes of this workbook. But, it is a topic that is critical in recovery and where recovering people have confusion or difficulty. I suggest that you speak to your therapist, sponsor or group members about sexual issues and follow their suggestions in this area. Consult the Resources section for more information on issues of sex and sexuality.

Let's review the potential benefits of Recreation as it relates to optimizing mental health and supporting recovery.

The Benefits of Recreation and Leisure Activities

1. Allows for creativity
2. Creates a sense of control and accomplishment
3. Creates a sense of freedom
4. Decreases stress and tension
5. Provides fun and pleasure
6. Gives a sense of personal well-being
7. Gives life balance
8. Healthy form of escape
9. Helps regulate sleeping and eating
10. Leads to self-discovery
11. Reduces boredom
12. Effective coping strategy
13. Laughter releases the "feel good" chemicals called endorphins

Leisure activities, play and laughter help to take the focus off of stress, troubles or whatever is worrying you. The shared experience with the other people who are involved in a game or adventure fosters a sense of belonging. If you have been feeling lonely or bored, choose something fun to do, invite a friend/friends and just do it! Be silly! Laugh a lot!

CHAPTER 5

Relationships: We Influence Each Other and We Need Each Other

Treasure your relationships, not your possessions.
—Anthony J. D'Angelo

The Reasons Why

Healthy relationships are an essential element of a fulfilled life. Philosophers, psychologists and scientists as well as the extensive research of Roger Walsh, M.D., PhD agree that the quality of our relationships is one of the most important of all lifestyle factors in determining the quality of our lives. They can be an immense force for good or a serious hindrance for recovering people.

Rich relationships lower the risk of disease ranging from the common cold to heart disease and strokes, and from psychological disorders such as depression. For those in recovery, it is essential to develop mutually supportive relationships with others who are supportive of your recovery.

Social neuroscience shows that we are hardwired for empathy and intimacy. Our brains resonate with one another like tuning forks, picking up subtle emotional and social cues, enabling us to empathize with others. We need one another, plain and simple: it's the human condition. Bonding with others affords us the opportunity to find purpose, feel connected, and experience feelings of safety.

Noted physician, Dr. Dean Ornish, has this to say about the importance of relationships to our mental health, "I am not aware of any other factor in medicine—not diet, not smoking, not exercise, not stress, not genetics, not drugs, not surgery—that has greater impact on our quality of life, incidence of illness, and premature death from all causes." Wow! That's quite a statement and a good reason to examine and clean up our relationships.

The list of researchers studying relationships and their importance to physical and mental health is long. There are endless self-help and professional programs for improving our relationship skills, and from all indications, this is an area that is most critical to optimizing resilience and mental health, so I recommend taking advantage of any of the offerings you can find in your area.

It is common for people in 12 Step programs to be advised to avoid changing their intimate relationship situations for a year after the beginning of sobriety. They are often told to avoid new romantic entanglements and to try not to disrupt current committed relationships until the year mark, to allow time for the brain to heal, judgment to improve, resentments to be cleared and some of the compulsive behaviors to wane. In this way, a more measured and mature approach can be taken to develop and sustain meaningful relationships. Because it is often true that people in recovery have sustained significant damage in their primary relationships, they long for something better and often run headlong into relationships that are initially soothing and gratifying, but suddenly become destructive and heart-breaking. I have sadly noticed that often the advice to wait is not taken seriously and is ignored, as the desperate search for the comfort of relationship is sought. The failure of a relationship is a prime time for relapse to occur. So, the reasons for the recommendation to wait are critical! To avoid further trauma, to have time to develop more maturity and better judgment, and make time to develop relationship skills outside a new romantic relationship. **Please wait!**

If you are currently single, have you been given the advice to wait a significant period of time before initiating a new romantic relationship? And, what is your willingness to follow this advice?

Chapter 5 | Relationships: We Influence Each Other and We Need Each Other

If not, why not?

If you are already married or in a committed relationship, will your partner support your recovery and tolerate your need to attend 12 Step meetings, meet with a sponsor and/or spiritual advisor, and generally spend a good bit of time on issues of recovery? If the answer is "no," how can you and your therapist/sponsor help your partner to understand that you may be less available than she/he had hoped for the first year of recovery?

According to Moran Cerf, a neuroscientist at Northwestern University who has been studying decision-making for many years, the surest way to maximize happiness and mental health has nothing to do with experiences, material goods, or personal philosophy. It's essentially about whom you choose to spend time with. His neuroscience research has found that when two people are in each other's company, their brain waves will begin to look identical. The more he studied relationships, the more he was able to see that just being next to certain people actually aligns your brain with theirs. In other words, we become more like the people we associate with … and they become more like us. Understanding this makes clear that carefully choosing whom you hang out with is critical to your mental health.

Who are your closest non-using friends/family?

If you are in residential treatment or an outpatient program, or trying sobriety on your own, will the people you live with be willing to keep your home alcohol and drug free? This doesn't mean that they cannot drink alcohol or use legally prescribed drugs; it just means that they will not keep alcohol or drugs in the house until sufficient time has elapsed for you to be solidly on your feet in recovery. Do you feel comfortable asking them to do this? Write a bit about this issue, and please don't tell me that this is not necessary. It may not be, but why take the chance?

If the answer is "no," please think about how you are valued in this relationship and what is necessary for you to have safety as you navigate recovery. Make some comments here regarding any thoughts you have about this.

Chapter 5 | Relationships: We Influence Each Other and We Need Each Other

Science journalist, Daniel Goleman, notes that our brain's very design makes it sociable, and inexorably drawn into an intimate brain-to-brain link-up whenever we engage with another person. That neural bridge lets us affect the brain—and so the body—of everyone we interact with, just as they do us. Among people around the world, nourishing relationships are the single most universally agreed upon feature of the good life.

Name three people you want to **be** more like, **think** more like, and who **inspire** your recovery. Tell me why you admire them.

1.

2.

3.

Write about the ways in which you believe that being with these three supports and inspires your recovery just by association.

What do you want in a close friend?

Do you have "sober" friends? "Normie" friends? Please describe here.

The various researchers tell us that good relationships with a variety of family, friends, co-workers, and partners improve our cognitive capacity and intelligence, increase our levels of happiness, and improve our general physical health and even longevity.

Chapter 5 | Relationships: We Influence Each Other and We Need Each Other

Unfortunately, social isolation is increasing, and began to increase with the advent of television and currently with endless hours spent on technology. When you have satisfactory relationships, you increase what is called your social capital. With current levels of social capital decreasing, relationships suffer and now more than ever you need to think about and cultivate better relationship skills. Make some notes about how many minutes/hours you spend with technology that could be spent in personal relationship.

Do you greet people you pass in the street or in the grocery store? _____

Would you consider trying it? _____ What happened? _____

It is a fact that our best healing takes place in community. The next time you hear someone say that they don't need help to stop drugs/drinking, they don't need a recovering community to relate to, just know that all the research says they are fooling themselves, because a recovering community is a great place to practice the art of conversation, listening and sharing, having patience and empathy, and so many other skills that are essential to relationship, but not easy to acquire as adults.

When researchers, including Roger Walsh, M.D., Dean Ornish, M.D., the Drs. John and Julie Gottman, tell us that satisfactory relationships are the number one, most important positive influence for mental health, what do they say about how to create them?

If you hope to improve all of your relationships, be they everyday friendships, business co-workers, or intimate relationships, look to the wisdom of John and Julie Gottman. When it comes to healthy relationships they are the Sages of our time, with their recommendations based on many years of scientific research in their so-called "Love Lab" at the University of Washington. And although they have focused their work on couples, their advice is generally suitable for most relationships. Everything they write about in their various books and articles is practical and can be put to immediate use. For example, one of their recommendations is found in two contrasting words, softness / harshness.

Soft starts and soft endings to our sentences are healthy, strong and healing. They lead to connection, respect and nurture. One of my teachers, David Cheek, M.D., told me, "Words are magic; they wound or they heal. Take your pick." The Gottmans have proven in their research that this is a fact.

Harsh starts and harsh endings to your sentences are unhealthy, weak and destructive. They typically lead to pain and drama. You must ask yourself, "Is my purpose to heal or wound?" Because your words will either be **neutral** or **healing** or **wounding** …. take your pick!

In addition, harsh words typically create drama and drama is ALWAYS an indulgence. So do not indulge yourself and avoid relationships that create or maintain drama.

Name-calling, blaming, accusing, controlling, humiliating the other, being unwilling to see or listen to another person's point of view, pouting, among other negative behaviors are all harsh and relationship killers. They are also immature and indicate that you may not be ready for relationships and are in need of better relationship skills.

Think about the family you grew up in (because they modeled relationship for you). Did you learn to be kind and loving there? Write a little about the general atmosphere in your original family. If you grew up with a parent/parents who were alcoholic or drug addicted, know that there are wonderful self-help books, as well as AlAnon and CODA for Adult Children of Alcoholics. Be sure to begin investigating this area of your history for clues about relationship issues you might have that need correcting.

Chapter 5 | Relationships: We Influence Each Other and We Need Each Other

_____
_____
_____
_____
_____
_____

Write a little about the person in your life who has taught you the most about managing a kind, respectful relationship.

_____
_____
_____
_____
_____
_____

With harsh words or aggressive behavior, the other person will feel attacked and respond defensively. There is no hope of healing with this approach and no helpful communication will occur.

A soft approach does not accuse or blame anyone; rather it is an invitation to a conversation between two equal adults. It allows each person to take responsibility for him/herself. If the person you are talking to becomes defensive, or if you become defensive, it means that one or both of you are not really listening for understanding of the other. Take a deep breath and try to listen for understanding, in which case, there is no need to be defensive.

Maintaining appropriate boundaries is essential to healthy relationship. Boundaries define what is and is not acceptable to you in your relationships.

There are many types of relationships. A few are: kinship, social, business, activity, collegial, transactional, intimate and romantic. How you communicate, share information about yourself, spend time with, and give of yourself depends upon your personal goals and how you want to live your life. When your boundaries are weak, unguarded, or unclear, you let in all sorts of people and experiences that aren't healthy. So, be discerning and have appropriate boundaries in your various relationships.

Clarity is the friend of healthy relationship. So, be crystal clear about your particular boundaries in relationships. For example, what are your boundaries about borrowing and lending money? What are your sexual boundaries? What are your boundaries about being on time or lateness? This list is endless and essential. So, think about your physical, sexual, verbal, financial, material, and any other categories you can think of that define your boundaries. This will take some time and effort, and it will be important to discern the boundaries of others to whom you relate. Remember, there are not necessarily right or wrong answers to these questions. Your boundaries are yours. When you know what they are, you can more easily negotiate relationships with others who may agree or disagree with you.

Use these pages to write about the various types of boundaries mentioned above and your thoughts about each.

Chapter 5 | Relationships: We Influence Each Other and We Need Each Other

Chapter 5 | Relationships: We Influence Each Other and We Need Each Other

Reciprocity is generally part of healthy Relationships. It means that we do for each other; the friendship or relationship is not a one-way street with one person doing all the giving or getting. There is no need to keep score on whom did what when. You can generally feel that the relationship is equally give and take. Write about your understanding of reciprocity in your relationships. Are you a giver? A taker? Or, is it mostly pretty even?

_____

_____

_____

_____

_____

_____

Because it is true that we become more like the company we keep, it is important that you choose people to hang out with who are more skilled in healthy relationship than you are. You will learn by observation and they can be a source of information and inspiration when you have questions about things like how to manage a disagreement with a friend, relative or partner, how to have better family relationships, how to be a better parent, etc. Who can you identify who can teach you about healthy relationships at home, in the workplace, and in the community? For example, if you want to learn more about long marriages, talk to people who have had long, satisfying marriages. If you want to have better work relationships, talk to someone who manages work well, etc. Sometimes people hold themselves out as experts in these areas, but have been unable to accomplish the very thing they are supposedly expert at. Look for teachers/mentors who have ACTUALLY accomplished what they claim to teach.

Write about who might help you learn more about relationship and boundaries in these various areas I have identified and any others you can think of. If you're not sure, how will you find these helpers? If you need more space, use the pages at the end of the workbook.

_____

_____

_____

Chapter 5 | Relationships: We Influence Each Other and We Need Each Other

Almost always, recovery means that relationships will change and some will go by the wayside. "Friends" who were drinking/using buddies must be relinquished. This can be a relief or it can be very painful. Let's hope that somewhere down the line they will catch the recovery train, too, and you can have a friendship in recovery. Until then, let them go. Really! Let them go! Make a list of the people that you must let go of and make note of how you feel about it.

Typically, our relationships with partners and family members will change. With whom in your family do you want to make changes in how you relate and how can you do that?

As you have read in this chapter, this TLC having to do with Relationship is vitally important to happiness and wellbeing. And yet, it is the place where most recovering people have great difficulty. It is common for people to relapse as the result of the stresses of a romantic relationship, which actually takes the most skill of all to navigate; thus, the advice given earlier to wait awhile before attempting a romantic relationship.

Relationships with family and friends have typically been damaged in addiction, and often the people who you have chosen to associate with have not been nurturing or healthy. So, a reworking of your entire field of relationships is probably in order. This is important enough to usually require the help of a good relationship therapist. So, ask around in the recovering community for some good referrals for this work, which extends to family, friends, co-workers, as well as partners.

Violence, whether verbal, emotional, physical or sexual, has no place in a healthy relationship and is actually a threat to mental health and recovery. If you are serious about your recovery, take a look at your own behavior in your relationships and determine if you are the aggressor. If so, please get professional help.

Do you fit a pattern of aggressor in relationships? Write about that.

If you are the victim, do not ever assume that your aggressor can change by him/herself, or with your help. Impossible! These are deeply ingrained relationship patterns and will take considerable professional help to change. Begin your escape from these relationship patterns with professional help. Are there aggressors who you should avoid? Write about that here.

_____

_____

_____

_____

_____

_____

_____

_____

Being able to enjoy healthy relationships requires the building of healthy relationship skills. The keys to building these skills lie in improving your own character over time. Character development is the work of a lifetime and I recommend long-term individual and group therapy as part of your healing journey. I know from research that long-term therapy improves the odds of maintaining sobriety and increasing your relationships skills. So, please find a good group therapist and stay a very long time.

Some of your self-discovery work may be very scary as you confront some unfortunate past behaviors, experiences and pain. With diligent work, you can accept who you once were, and who you are today. Hopefully, you will eventually find forgiveness for yourself for past behavior and hold yourself accountable to a newly developed set of healthy boundaries and relationship skills. Self-awareness is key in healthy relationship. Being able to see your own part in challenging situations and correcting it to the best of your ability makes room for possible repair.

Learning how to select and nurture relationships is a skill in and of itself. This is critically important.

Possible Actions for Implementation

- Read books on Boundaries and practice communicating them
- Take an "Education for Marriage" class through a local church or attend pre-marital counseling if you are getting married, or marriage counseling if you are already partnered
- Enroll in communications classes at your local community college.
- Read self-help books about Relationships
- Practice "soft starts" during challenging communication
- Learn about others by asking questions about them
- Make a new friend who is somewhat different from you (a different race, religion, socio-economic level, profession, etc.)
- Read any of the Gottman's books on Relationship
- Make a habit of remembering people's birthdays and other important events in their lives
- Be a good friend to yourself, taking good care of yourself

Your Ideas

Write a bit about what you know about your relationship patterns that have to do with YOU. Start by noting the repeating patterns of relationship in your life, as you are able to identify them.

What are the things you do in relationships that seem to work well?

_____

_____

_____

_____

_____

_____

What are the things you do in relationships that do not work well and are in need of change?

_____

_____

_____

_____

_____

_____

Addiction sickens and eventually will kill self-esteem and relationships. What once may have been an attempt at socializing and having fun has become a spoiler of both. Metaphorically speaking, addiction harms your Self and traps you in slavery.

Acknowledging your past honestly will help you stop doing things that cause damage, hurt or pain to yourself and others and begin a better life. When you do your 4th Step in a 12 Step program, you will be able to better identify your own behaviors that have harmed your relationships. People often approach a 4th Step with trepidation, but with the firm, but loving guidance of your sponsor, you will find valuable information and relief. It will give you an opportunity to identify some of your relationship killing behavior and the possibility of making changes, as you choose.

Have you done a 4th Step? If not, are you concerned about it? If you have completed a 4th Step, what did you learn about your relationship patterns?

If you are not in a 12 Step program, you can still take an inventory of your relationships and determine your part in harming them or being harmed by them. It is important to learn from your past behavior that has been destructive, and also learn who it is in your life that supports your recovery or detracts from it.

If you are in early recovery, a pet can provide some of the affection, pleasure and entertainment that you are longing for. Animals provide love, help you learn about yourself, build relationships with other people and encourage responsibility. While you may have lost the trust of loved ones and friends due to your addiction, a pet is loyal and will respond to affection. Having the responsibility for another living creature is a fantastic way to encourage discipline and responsibility on a daily basis.

No matter what kind of animal you choose, pets can be a great comfort as well as fun and accompany you on your healing journey.

Do you have a pet? If so, please describe.

Benefits of Healthy Relationships

- Learn, mature and see new possibilities
- Strengthen emotions and social interactions with others
- Share ideas, advice, experiences in confidence
- Support and help each other heal
- Share love and caring
- Assist in reducing conflicts and meeting challenges
- Provide a buffer against stress
- Be healthier and live longer
- Experience more life satisfaction

Conversely, the health risks from being isolated or in unhealthy relationships can contribute to depression, decreased immune function, anxiety, anger, higher blood pressure, and obesity.

Good friends can be good medicine. Since this TLC has been identified as the most important of all eight, be sure to spend sufficient time and effort to sort out this area of your life. Understand that good relationships require time, effort and reciprocity. Choose wisely, as you become like the company you keep. It will be well worth the time, effort and money spent!

CHAPTER 6
Time in Nature

Nature is God's reset button for our minds, bodies, and spirits.
—Michael Hyatt

The Reasons Why

Time in Nature, though proven to be a great healing force, has become a luxury for many of us living in the Western industrialized world. Think of it! Unlike our grandparents and farther back ancestors, we are living mostly indoors under artificial lighting, in manufactured environments. In 1900, only 15% of the world's population lived in urban areas. The remaining 85% lived in rural areas, where nature was everywhere around. By some estimates, by 2050, over 70% of the world's population will live in urban settings, removed from much of the naturally occurring world.

Some psychologists and educators have called this state of affairs Post-Nature Deficit Disorder. They say that modern people, by cutting themselves off from nature, have cut themselves off from the nature of their own being, because we humans are a part of nature, too, and dependent on it.

Whether we're in our homes, cars, or offices, we spend most of our days removed from nature—and it's proving not to be good for us. Research consistently supports the connection between getting active outside and improved psychological health, where stress, anxiety, anger, and gloom diminish, and optimism, self-esteem, and vitality increase. By contrast, walking through a shopping mall has been shown to raise stress and lower self-esteem. This shouldn't be surprising given our million years or so of evolution out in the natural world. Since the 1980s we have spent 90-95% of our time indoors—a first in human history.

It turns out that our mothers were onto something when they told us to turn off the TV or the video games and "go outside and play."

Many people relate to the notion that a particular aspect of the natural world is "my special place," or a place that helped shape them. It can be the mountains, the forests, the waterways, the open spaces of meadows or grasslands, the deserts, or some other place. In the space below, write about this special place and it's meaning for you. If you haven't identified your favorite place in nature, think about a pleasant memory that took place outdoors and write about that.

Nowadays, how often are you able to spend time in this particular place, or somewhere similar?

There are many psychological, physical, and spiritual benefits to connecting to the natural world. Recovering people in particular, and people in general, find that regular contact with nature is beneficial. Time spent outdoors leads to relief from stress, increased attention and awareness, experiences of trust and reduced need for control, and is one of the most common triggers for peak spiritual experiences. I recall a man in my care, who was a combat veteran and based on his wartime experience, had become an avowed atheist. He arrived at the construction site where he would work that day, quite early in the morning. As he sat, drinking his coffee quietly in his truck, he saw a mountain lion walking across the field in front of him. "In that sacred moment, I knew that God existed and lived in nature," he said.

Emotional numbing is one possible result of nature deficit and it means that you have no emotional response to something that would ordinarily cause you to have a feeling of some sort. If you are not outdoors, then you have no experience of the joy and awe of seeing aspects of the beauty of nature. Buzzing bees, the intricacies of flowers, the majesty of trees, and the crash of ocean waves are all there to delight your senses, if only you are outdoors to witness them.

Likewise, you may have no sadness or anger at the pollution that is in the oceans and waterways, the trash by the side of the road and the destruction of the habitats of our animal friends. Their suffering is far removed from you if you are never outdoors to witness to it.

Do you see any symptoms of emotional numbing in yourself? Please write about what that here.

Our always *on*, never-disconnected way of living robs us of the rejuvenation that the God of our understanding intended us to regularly experience in the natural world. Though amazing technological advances have enabled us to live in urban environments and lightened the loads of physical labor by mostly working indoors at desks, or with the help of automation in outdoor jobs, it has been at a considerable physical and psychological cost as we have distanced from the natural world that sustains us. This disconnection affects us in multiple ways and has ultimately led to the degradation of the earth that is threatening our very survival. This is an important aspect of *Time in Nature*, because typically, the more we notice the natural world around us, the birds, the trees and plants, the squirrels, deer, raccoons and other woodland creatures, the more we tend to care about the preservation of nature in all its forms, which is also about our own survival.

Write about the aspects of nature that you most enjoy and how you feel when you see, hear, smell or otherwise experience them.

Living in the world of media … a world of images and dialogue, which can be interesting and expansive, comes at the cost of your own personal experience out in the world. The natural world is the real world.

How much time do you spend on media (television, computer, cell phone, etc.) compared to being outdoors? Give the ratio if you can.

Chapter 6 | Time in Nature

How nature-deficient are you? Do you have "Nature Deficit Disorder?" Reconnecting with the great outdoors can help lift depression, improve energy, and boost overall feelings of wellbeing and mental health. Being in nature has long been associated with being mindful and meditative, but only recently has the scientific community researched the mental health benefits of outdoor immersion. It delivers not only health benefits, but also wider social benefits and cost savings that medication does not. Active, social and adventurous contact with nature may be combined with other interventions to protect and enhance your health and wellbeing, as well as contributing to the treatment of chronic mental, emotional and physical health difficulties. Although an hour a day is better, even spending just 20 minutes outside per day can boost your energy levels and produce a greater sense of vitality.

Realistically, how much time do you believe you can spend outdoors on a regular basis? During the week? On the weekend?

_____

_____

_____

_____

_____

_____

Consciously incorporating a natural environmental component into your holistic therapeutic lifestyle changes makes sense for people in recovery. The benefits of nature for body, mind and soul are finding their way to prescription pads, too, as more healthcare providers are telling their patients to take a hike – literally. Doctors and therapists give their patients "nature prescriptions" to help treat a variety of medical conditions, from alcoholism and drug abuse to post-cancer fatigue, obesity, high blood pressure, diabetes, and mental health disorders.

Two so-called eco-therapies that are often used in inpatient and outpatient treatment settings that reconnect you with the rest of nature are animal assisted therapy and horticultural therapy. There is no doubt that creating relationships of trust, kindness and playfulness with animals is a healing experience. Likewise, creating beauty in nature, through gardening, whether for food or flowers, requires patience, responsibility and following directions. These have increasingly been proven to be effective ways of relieving the loneliness and disconnection experienced by many people, and especially those who have suffered from addiction or any form of mental illness. In the space below, please write about either or both of these two interventions … time with animals and/or time gardening, and how it might be possible to incorporate one of these into your overall program of recovery. Don't forget that gardening can take place with potted plants if you don't have a yard to work in, and that working with indoor plants counts, too.

In this space, write about your favorite experience with an animal:

In this space, write about your best experience growing something for food or beauty:

Chapter 6 | Time in Nature

How can nature help you avoid relapse and have a healthier life? Years of research have confirmed evidence that eco or green therapy has regenerative powers, improving mood and easing anxiety, stress, and depression that often accompany addiction. Reconnection with the natural world is a freely available activity that can help you heal and thrive. Being in nature, or even viewing scenes of nature, reduces anger, fear, and stress, and increases pleasant feelings. Exposure to nature contributes to your physical wellbeing, reducing blood pressure, heart rate, muscle tension, and the production of stress hormones. In addition, nature helps us cope with pain. The health effects of green space are wide-ranging, and show strong associations between access to nature and longer, healthier lives.

Researchers at the University of Illinois discovered that green outdoor spaces relieve the symptoms of Attention Deficit Disorder; the greener the setting, the more the relief. By contrast, indoor activities, such as watching television or playing on paved, non-green areas, increase the symptoms of ADD. In a similar vein, MacArthur Genius Award recipient, Majora Carter, in her work nicknamed, *Greening the Ghetto*, found research indicating that where there are trees and vegetation in neighborhoods, crime is reduced. She started planting trees and building bike paths and parks in her inner city neighborhood in New York for the health and wellbeing of the community. Clearly, time in nature has a large impact on our moods and behaviors if it can even reduce the crime rate.

In the space below, name several places within easy walking distance of your treatment center, home and workplace where you can spend time in nature.

_____

_____

_____

_____

_____

_____

A chapter on *Time in Nature* would not be complete without mentioning Vitamin D as an important nutrient for healing. Getting enough of this vitamin, which is possibly actually a hormone is critical to maintaining a healthy immune system and sunlight is the means of getting it. Vitamin D forms right on your skin when you are outdoors. Though you can take Vitamin D supplements, its best to get it from natural sources, meaning the sun! By helping maximize calcium absorption, Vitamin D promotes bone and dental health. It can also elevate mood and reduce the risk of cancer, heart disease, Alzheimer's, stroke, diabetes, and more. Vitamin D also improves blood flow and lowers blood pressure by literally relaxing your blood vessels. While we all know to protect ourselves from the sun to avoid skin cancer, we also need vitamin D for bone growth, cell growth, inflammation reduction and neuromuscular and immune function. "Sensible sun exposure" means only going out in the sun for about one third to one half of the amount of time it would take your skin to mildly burn, or roughly 10 to 15 minutes for many. After you've gotten a bit of vitamin D, reach for the sunscreen and continue your exploration of the great outdoors.

Spending too much time inside, away from natural light and with increased exposure to artificial light can alter your circadian rhythms, thus disrupting your sleep pattern. Your internal body clock is naturally tied to the sun's schedule. Early morning exposure to sunlight has been shown to help recalibrate these sleep cycles. A few consecutive days outside on a fishing or backpacking trip will get the job done much faster. Natural light normalizes your sleep schedule by assisting in the regulation of the melatonin system, and sound, uninterrupted sleep is essential to recovery. Difficulty sleeping is a big component of addiction and other mental health problems. Write about your quality of sleep. Is it such that you wake up rested? Do you need more outdoor time to ease any sleep problems?

_____

_____

_____

_____

_____

_____

_____

Your body has to work hard to get the oxygen it needs to function in polluted or indoor environments. This raises your heart rate and blood pressure. As you learned in the chapter on Relaxation, breathing techniques have the ability to dampen the production of stress hormones as well as train your body's reaction to stressful situations. Rapid breathing engages your body's sympathetic nervous system (or, your "fight or flight, freeze" response), which is activated by stress and works to energize the body. Slow, deep breathing—the kind encouraged by the great outdoors—stimulates the body's parasympathetic reaction, which calms us down. Whether you are running on a fitness trail or just looking at trees at a playground, you can reduce your blood pressure as well as the stress-related hormones cortisol and adrenaline.

"Forest bathing," so named by the Japanese, are trips into the woods for ninety minutes or more, that can significantly decrease your anxiety, depression, anger, confusion and fatigue. And because stress inhibits the immune system, the stress-reduction benefits of being among the trees are further magnified. But, remember, even just five minutes in a garden, park, or green golf course may improve your short-term working memory and overall health.

Spending time in nature has been linked to improved attention spans (short and long term), boosts in serotonin (the feel good neurotransmitter) and shows increased activity in the parts of the brain responsible for empathy, emotional stability, and love (whereas urban environments do the same for fear and anxiety). If you're feeling down, get outside.

Our lives are busier than ever with jobs, school, meetings and family life. Trying to focus on many activities or even a single thing for long periods of time can mentally drain you, a phenomenon called "Directed Attention Fatigue." Spending time in the outdoors, looking at plants, water, birds, mountains, and other aspects of nature gives the cognitive, thinking portion of the brain a break, allowing you to focus better and renew your ability to be present and patient. Whether you are hiking, gardening, birding, building sand castles, or simply sitting and observing, nature provides opportunities to relax and refresh and improve focus and concentration

Elements of the environment, such as the smell of the wood, the sound of a running stream of water, and the vibrant colors of the forest can provide relaxation and reduce stress, which may lower your levels of cortisol, pulse rate, and blood pressure. Physicians and psychologists have long known that sunlight is a good treatment for seasonal affective disorder (SAD). There's a world of benefit to being out in nature and I want you to have it as a regular part of your recovery program.

Do you have a natural setting you can retreat to when you feel stressed? Where do you go and what do you like about it?

What natural items (for example, plants, animals, shells, rocks, feathers, artwork) have you brought indoors into your living space to remind you of the natural world?

What you focus your mind on when you are outdoors is important. Clear your mind of any thoughts other than what you are seeing and experiencing. Focus on the sights, sounds and smells around you to relax your mind. You'll return from your *Time in Nature* refreshed and ready for other activities of the day.

Possible Actions for Implementation

Find your own meaning in the natural world and the adventures you experience there. Here are some activities you can start incorporating into your everyday life, as well as some possible assignments for time in nature:

1. Take a 20-minute walk outdoors every day. During your walk, focus on the various aspects of nature that you encounter and keep a journal of what you observe. How many birds or other critters did you see? How many trees did you pass and what kind were they? Did you see flowers? If so, what colors and kinds did you see? The point is to be truly present for your time in nature in a way that allows you to appreciate the experience.

2. Walk your dog or offer to walk someone else's dog on a new route from time to time and observe new surroundings. It's nice to have a companion on your outdoor adventures.

3. Sit outdoors and simply observe for 20 minutes. Notice what you see, what you smell, what you feel (the sun or rain on your face), and what you hear during that time and remember the moment and/or write about it.

4. If you live near the ocean where there are tide pools, take a magnifying glass to them and see what you can see.

5. Find a tree that you like and observe the patterns of the bark. Be able to describe it in your journal, i.e., color, texture, pattern, smell. What does it feel like to hug a tree? Go ahead! Do it!

6. Spend time gardening. If it is winter or you don't live where this is a possibility, bring nature inside by planting a windowsill herb garden, or tend other indoor plants.

7. Combine time in nature with other areas of *8 Ways*, such as exercising outdoors, climbing hills, playing outdoor sports with friends, taking a nap outdoors at the beach, flying a kite, picnicking in the woods with your family, or volunteering in local clean-up activities.

8. Choose one aspect of nature to focus on. Let's say you have decided to observe an ant colony today. As you observe the ants at work, ask yourself what they can teach you about recovery and life in general. What is the metaphor for your own life that is in progress as you observe? Write your observations in your journal. Taking lessons from nature is a powerful exercise!

9. Find an outdoor labyrinth and walk it.

10. If you want to feel the energy of earth, lie down on the grass or sand, or go barefoot at the beach or park. The earth has a magnetic field and you can feel it if you are still enough and there is quiet. Bringing your body into the same frequency as that magnetic field is called "grounding." Grounding can have an intense anti-inflammatory and energizing effect on the body. Nature's calming effect comes from not only the fresh air, but also the ground.

Your Ideas

I've given you some ideas for your time in nature. In the space below write a few more possibilities that reflect things you could do that would be enjoyable to you and that you are likely to actually do. Be a little adventurous! Try to add activities in nature that enrich your everyday experience of life and reignite whatever interest you have had in the natural world, of which you are an integral part! Try to get at least five more suggestions to add to mine.

1.

2.

3.

4.

5.

Use this chart to schedule *Time in Nature* each day for the next seven days, along with your experience. There are more pages for you to extend this charting at the end of this workbook in Appendix A.

Nature Activity	Location	Time Spent	Feelings/Sensations/ Mood Before	Feelings/Sensations/ Mood After

Benefits of Time in Nature

- Accelerates recovery from surgery or illness
- Alleviates mental fatigue
- Boosts fitness if combined with Exercise
- Boosts self-confidence
- Boosts immune function
- Clears the mind
- Enhances cognitive function
- Enlivens your senses
- Essential for healthy aging
- Fuels imagination
- Improves mood
- Improves sleep
- Increases the ability to focus, even in children
- Increases energy level
- Increases your awareness
- Lowers blood pressure
- Reduces stress
- Reduces symptoms of depression

When we spend more **Time in Nature,** we are more willing to participate in its preservation. Environmental concerns are at critical proportions. When you are aware of your natural world environment, you will become more conscious of your own impact and hopefully become a better steward of this beautiful outdoors that has been gifted to us by our Creator.

CHAPTER 7
Giving Back

*"We make a living by what we get,
but we make a life by what we give."*
— Winston Churchill

The Reasons Why

Giving from our abundance is a proven way to increase our feelings of self-worth and self-confidence. So often, the experience of addiction has robbed us of any feeling of generosity or a balanced and regular practice of giving. It does not mean that you are inherently selfish. It means that in the throws of addiction you are in a state of consciousness in which it is difficult to access the more altruistic parts of yourself. Some recovering people cannot imagine that they have anything worth giving, that no one would want what they have to offer.

It is often said that addiction is a selfish disease, and so part of the antidote to that disease is to reverse the feeling of "never enough." People who are suffering, and/or simply focused on finding their next drink or drug do not generally have the mental energy to think about altruism, or the physical energy to devote to it.

Most people have a desire to be helpful to others. Not only does it feel good to uplift others or contribute to the community in some way, it adds to a sense of meaning and shifts our energy from loneliness and separation to joy and connection.

12-Step programs emphasize "getting a commitment," which typically means volunteering for one of any number of tasks before, during and after meetings, such as being a greeter, setting up chairs, making coffee, arranging a literature table, or cleaning up afterwards. Sponsors usually make getting a commitment a recommendation or requirement early on in their sponsoring of a newcomer. There is wisdom behind this suggestion, as research supports **Giving Back** as one of the **8 Ways to Wellbeing**.

Roger Walsh, M.D., in his book, *Essential Spirituality,* suggests that when beginning to nurture a nature of generosity, it is important to start small. He says to look for small ways of giving to others with no expectation of getting anything in return. It is often a habit of recovering people to overdo, perhaps from guilt, or trying to make up for lost time, or simply not having much experience with estimating time and energy allotments for these new practices. Dr. Walsh quotes Mother Teresa, who urged, "Don't look for spectacular actions. What is important is the gift of yourself. It is the degree of love you insert in your deeds." So, starting small is good advice, and remembering to add the love, is essential.

In addition, Dr. Walsh advises finding ways to give that you enjoy. If you find volunteer activities and opportunities that you enjoy, you are more likely to continue doing them. Sometimes this requires experimentation because you may not know what sort of volunteering will be enjoyable. Be adventurous and try some different volunteer activities and see what fits. You might like volunteering to bathe dogs at your local Humane Society, or playing with the animals there so that they remain socialized and more likely to be adopted. People in nursing homes enjoy visitors, and your local library has a literacy program where you can volunteer to teach an adult to read or re-shelve books. Community organizations of all sorts are always looking for volunteers for a variety of tasks. At the same time, small acts, such as phoning a relative who hasn't heard from you in a while, just to say hi, definitely counts, as does holding the door for someone, walking their dog or offering to babysit for an hour or two while your friend grocery shops. Do what you can, but make it a habit.

Giving Back is a proven means to good health and happiness. The practice of gratitude through giving back can be transformational in supporting recovery, re-entering the world as a person in recovery, and sustaining long-term wellness. In a recent speech, Dr. Joycelyn Elders, our former U.S. Surgeon General, said, "When the ladder has been lowered down so that you can climb up, be sure to lower that ladder again, so that the next person can climb up, too." Certainly, the 12th Step of 12 Step programs supports this value, when it states, "Having had a spiritual awakening as the result of following these steps, we tried to carry this message to alcoholics ….." The idea, of course, is to give back or "pay forward," what has so generously been given to you.

I believe that many of the maladies of today's society have to do with a general lack of meaning to our lives and a self-centered focus. Turning your gaze outside yourself, and beginning to contribute to the world's work can start a process of expanded awareness of the world around you, and the ways in which you can make a difference in that world. Certainly this mindset has the potential to improve your relationships with others and increase your own self-esteem. Do you remember when President John F. Kennedy, in his famous speech said, "Ask not what your country can do for you. Ask what you can do for your country?" Well, I am suggesting the same thing, but I am expanding on that thought to suggest that when you offer up your help and support of others, whether they are human, animal or the natural environment, you are doing something that improves your own functioning too. The exciting thing about this concept is that as you contribute to the world's work, you can experience the joy of service as you develop your character and your leadership skills in a positive way. It is a worthwhile inquiry to consider the ways in which you are meant to be of service in this world. Tommy Rosen, a well-known yoga teacher and advocate of service in recovery says, "Once you find your means of service, the keys to the kingdom are in your hands."

In the space below, list three ideas you have for giving back or volunteering in your home, place of worship, community or elsewhere.

_____

_____

_____

_____

_____

Giving Back helps the giver by reducing painful, unhealthy emotional states such as greed, jealousy, and egocentricity, while strengthening pleasant, healthy emotional states such as happiness, joy and generosity. This is very important because it is common for recovering people to experience significant depression and/or anxiety as part of what are known as post-acute withdrawal symptoms. Other symptoms such as restlessness, mood swings, irritability, fatigue, variable energy, disturbed sleep, low enthusiasm and variable concentration can be part of this picture. Post-acute withdrawal can last a very long time, even months or years. While we know that exercise, good nutrition and the rest of the healthy habits of therapeutic lifestyle choices are important, the mood altering effects of doing something for someone else is one means of addressing the challenges of recovery and ultimately leads to a more meaningful life.

In the space below, list any symptoms of post-acute withdrawal that you experience.

_____

_____

_____

_____

_____

_____

_____

_____

There is a certain self-discipline that comes of Giving Back and self-discipline is important for recovering people. Giving Back means that I am using some of my precious time and resources to do something for someone else. It means that I must give up or let go of that time, money, or whatever I'm giving, as a service for the betterment of another. So, I am going to make a sacrifice of my time, what is convenient or expedient for me, and possibly, my resources. In this process, I will learn to be more focused on the good of the larger community, as opposed to, "what I want right now." I will also need to plan my daily or weekly schedule in a way that allows for my area of service.

Children's Defense Fund founder, Marian Wright Edelman says, "Service is the rent we pay for the life we have been given." If you have been given the gift of recovery, never mind the great gift of life itself, then your service is certainly your repayment. Since you live every day in the company of others and the larger society, it is important to do your part to create an atmosphere of kindness and generosity. Generosity usually leads to more generosity. Those of you who participate in acts of kindness and caring behavior are creating a kinder and more caring atmosphere in which to live and work.

Contributions and service to others can produce a potent euphoria or "helper's high." The neural "glow" from paying it forward even shows up on MRI scans of the brain. This feel-good sensation is experienced at a cellular level that boosts everything from your psychological outlook to heart health and a robust immune system. Altruism benefits both physical and mental health and can even extend the lifespan.

In the space below, list the last act of service that you performed and what you experienced as a result.

_____

_____

_____

Clearly, generosity and service to others improves physical and mental health. But, it is also a component of the teachings and philosophies of every major religion. Most spiritual traditions emphasize service as a means to, and expression of, psychological and spiritual health and maturity. Dr. Walsh points out that, "Jewish tradition holds that each of us carries a spark of the Divine within us. Jesus called those who follow his example, 'the light of the world,' while Basque shamans describe human beings as walking stars." Spiritual maturity means you are mastering the therapeutic lifestyle change of Giving Back.

Let generosity go viral!

Possible Actions for Implementation

There are hundreds of ways of displaying goodwill and generosity. Even the smallest gesture can improve someone else's day as well as your own. What follows is a list of just a very few possibilities for **Giving Back**:

- Play an instrument and/or sing at a senior citizen center
- Volunteer in a classroom or Scout troop
- Teach someone to read and write through the local library literacy program
- Wash dogs at your local Humane Society
- Send a greeting card to a friend or relative
- Pick up litter and deposit it in a trash can
- Drive a cancer patient to treatment

- Serve on a phone bank for your political party
- Read to a child
- Volunteer at a 12 Step meeting
- Work in a community garden
- Organize a walking group of 2 or more friends
- Donate clothing, music, books and items you don't use
- Collect canned goods for the local food pantry
- Ride, walk or run for a cause
- Start a lending library or book club
- Visit patients in a VA or nursing home
- Volunteer with Mothers Against Drunk Drivers, Friends Against Drunk Driving
- Take meals to shut-ins through *Meals on Wheels*
- Play sports with kids with special needs
- Open the door for someone
- Contact Volunteers of America (VOA) to find a placement in your area of interest
- Smile at others and offer a compliment while looking them in the eye
- Volunteer in your place of worship
- Write a personal note of gratitude to someone
- Offer to babysit for a friend's children
- Give food coupons to a homeless person
- Treat a friend or relative to coffee, a meal or a movie
- Call your mother or other relative and ask how they are doing
- Offer to take someone's dog for a walk
- Make muffins for your neighbor—whether you know them or not

My mother used to say, "All things in moderation." Moderation and reality are key elements in making health-enhancing decisions. To be strong for others, you need to be strong. Manage your expectations. You can't do everything and not everyone will be grateful for what you do. If you begin to feel resistance or resentment, step back and ask yourself if you are doing too much or expecting praise for your generosity. If so, check your motives!

When I asked His Holiness the 14th Dalai Lama about this topic, He instructed that one meditate on why one was choosing to do a particular activity. If the answer emerges that you had been told you ought to do it, or should do it, that would be a wrong reason. He advised to do it because you believe it is the right thing to do. Of course, this doesn't mean that you don't take advice from others. But, the advice you are given should be examined and followed only if it seems like the right thing to do.

Giving to others does not mean distracting yourself from your goals or depleting your energy. Helping others is not a substitute or excuse for not helping yourself. Don't take on too much, too fast. Start slow. Fulfilling your commitments of talent, time or money is important, as others will rely on you to do what you said you would do. Keep in mind that following through on things is a healthy habit. By incorporating these eight healthy lifestyle choices into your daily living, you are following through on your promise to yourself and significant others that you will value your recovery, and become and remain trustworthy and truthful. So, don't over promise and under deliver. You can always increase your involvement once you know what you can do without needlessly stressing yourself or neglecting your recovery plan. Take on one thing at a time and give it your best.

Ways I currently help others:	Frequency (daily, monthly, etc.)
1.	
2.	
3.	
4.	
5.	

I help/don't help others because:

Your Ideas

Five Things I can do this week to **Give Back**. There are more pages for you to write on at the end of this workbook.

Helping Act	For Whom	Where	When	How I Felt After

Benefits of Giving Back

- Strengthens your recovery and grounds you in recovery principles
- Gives meaning/purpose to your life
- Helps you discover and enhance your strengths
- Prevents isolation
- Keeps you active
- Helps cultivate gratitude
- Helps to work through guilt, regret and other negative emotions

- Increases self-esteem
- Stimulates the development of new career and social skills
- Builds confidence in your abilities
- Ignites new passions
- Extends life
- Increases happiness
- Expands circle of contacts, friends and associates
- Releases natural feel-good chemicals in the brain (endorphins, serotonin, dopamine, and oxytocin)

You have received the great gift of life! Use your gift to enhance the lives of others and the world around you. When its time for you to leave this life, you will have created a legacy of goodness and your ancestors will smile.

CHAPTER 8
Spirituality

We are not humans on a spiritual path.
Rather, we are spirits on a human path.
— Jean Shinoda Bolen, MD

The Reasons Why

The 2nd Step in all 12 Step programs says, "We came to believe that a power greater than ourselves could restore us to sanity." The 3rd Step says, "We made a decision to turn our will and our lives over to the care of God as we understood Him."

Whether you follow a 12 Step program of recovery or not, a Spiritual life is shown by Dr. Walsh's research to be a cornerstone of the *8 Ways to Wellbeing* and the foundation of a healthy life.

Religion and spirituality are vitally important to most people in the world. Some 90% of the world's population engages in religious and spiritual practices. Religious and spiritual beliefs are an important part of dealing with life's joys and hardships. Faith communities at their best can provide a sense of purpose and guidelines for living a moral life and character development. Among recovering people who have been introduced to a 12 Step program, it is the 2nd and 3rd Step that begin the process of developing a spiritual practice, which will hopefully evolve, grow and deepen as time and recovery continue.

In most healing traditions, and in the beginnings of Western medicine, concerns of the body and spirit were intertwined. Over time, with the scientific revolution and growth of a medical model and pharmacology, these considerations were ignored or diminished.

Today, however, a growing number of studies reveal that spirituality may play a bigger role in the recovery process than previously acknowledged by physicians and scientists. We've learned that the body, mind and spirit are connected and cannot really be separated ... each influences the other. The health of any one of these elements seems to affect the others.

Spirituality includes a belief in a power operating in the universe that is greater than oneself, a sense of interconnectedness with all living creatures, an awareness of the purpose and meaning of life and the development of personal values. It's the way we find meaning, cope, are comforted, and have inner peace and reverence for life in all its forms.

There is abundant evidence that the potential for religious or spiritual experience resides in everyone. Spirituality is part of your birthright! How you access and practice this is up to you and must fit with your values and belief system.

Spirituality has enormous healing potential. What seems to be helpful is an inner personal commitment to faith/spirituality and/or religious practice.

Medical studies indicate that spiritual people are less prone to self-destructive behaviors and have less stress, less depression, less physical disability and a greater total life satisfaction. Spirituality can reduce depression, improve blood pressure, decreases muscle tension, lowers respiratory and heart rates and boosts the immune system. People in recovery find their religious beliefs and/or spiritual practices can help them fight feelings of helplessness, restore meaning and order to life situations, and help them regain a sense of control. High levels of hope and optimism, key factors in fighting depression and controlling urges, were found among those who regularly practiced their faith.

Obviously, the benefits of spiritual practice span an array of health measures. People call on their religion or spiritual concepts when faced with illness as well as emotional and physical stress for help and support. Increased resilience, better relationships and marriages are also attributed to regular religious and/or spiritual involvement.

The most amazing result seems to be on lifespan. Strikingly, Dr. Walsh's research showed that people who attend religious services weekly tend to live seven years longer than those who don't, even when baseline health and behaviors have been statistically controlled.

Noted psychologist and author, Charlotte Kasl, Ph.D., wrote an expanded version of several of the 12 Steps, which I offer here. For Step 2, she wrote, "We come to believe that God/The Goddess/Universe/Great Spirit/Higher Power awakens the healing wisdom within us when we open ourselves to that power." She says that this step, "affirms that a sacred spirit or life force energy is within us and around us. We tap into the power of the universe, draw it in and use it to awaken our inner capacity for healing. We are not separated isolated beings, we are part of One Energy, connected to the vast universe. Thus it is important that we develop our capacity to be touched by nature and beauty. We learn to see the wonder in small things—from a new leaf to a child's smile."

Say something here about your own understanding of Higher Power.

Now write your own version of Step 2

She goes on to offer as part of a 3rd Step expansion, "We make a decision to find our authentic selves and trust in the healing power of the truth. Instead of adopting society's inauthentic stereotypes, this step encourages us to reach deep and ask ourselves: Who am I? What do I feel? What is my experience? What feels right for me? What are my dreams, and strengths? Experiencing the healing power of the truth is about minute-to-minute honesty with oneself and others. It's about what you wear, what you eat, and being able to say, Yes, No and Maybe, without justifying yourself or undue worry about what the other person will think or say. It's about being *true* to oneself without guilt. It also affirms that human relations, intimacy and power are grounded in hearing and speaking our truths, simply, kindly and without apology. Ultimately being close to the bones of truth is what creates intimacy, trust, feelings of connection, and a quiet mind. This is truly integral to a spiritual way of life."

What things in your life give you a sense of inner peace, comfort, strength, love and connection? This is part of the truth of who you are. Please write about it here.

Who are the people that you get caught up in worrying about in terms of what they think of you? Who do you worry about pleasing?

Spiritual wellness is a personal matter involving values and beliefs that provide a purpose in your life. While different individuals may have different views of what spirituality is, it is generally considered to be the search for meaning and purpose in human existence, leading one to strive for a state of harmony with oneself and others while working to balance inner needs with the rest of the world. For most people, religion and spirituality are especially important in coping with stress and illness, and are beneficial to those in recovery. Authentic spirituality holds us together in our darkest moments, days or weeks. It is anything that leads us toward, or contributes to, or maintains our health. It gives us the strength and confidence to admit our mistakes, focus on our strengths and offer mercy and forgiveness to ourselves, and others.

So, let's talk for a minute about the difference between spiritual life and religion. Religions have been shown to be a powerful force for good in the lives of many people when the religion is inclusive, tolerant of other paths and emphasizes kindness, love, gratitude and forgiveness, as opposed to fear and judgment. Religions tend to have a particular set of ethics, customs, beliefs, and ceremonies. All of this can be a wonderful means of sharing in a community of common faith. A good rule of thumb is to remember if you were raised in a particular religion and recall whether or not it was meaningful to you. If so, I recommend that if you are not currently practicing this religion, and if it is not a shaming/blaming one, then why not revisit it for a few weeks (not just once) to see if it might fit into a spiritual practice now. Give it a chance! If it works for you, well good. If not, you have a choice to keep shopping for a religious institution that is more comfortable for you, or go your own way (which is actually harder, but doable).

I belonged to a club in high school that made a special project of visiting the religious institutions of every girl in the club. Since there were twenty-five members, we visited many places of worship. It was a fabulous experience and I highly recommend it. Visiting places of worship is a good way to broaden your spiritual horizons, and you just might find a spiritual home.

What places of worship/religions have you been exposed to or have you investigated?

_____

_____

_____

_____

_____

Which of the above (if any) intrigued you or made you want to return?

_____

_____

_____

_____

Chapter 8 | Spirituality

Religions typically provide a weekly spiritual practice of ceremony, prayer, inspirational messages, singing, etc. If it touches your heart, it is the easiest way to develop spiritual practice. If you decided to visit a religious service, write about what happened and how you felt about it.

Sadly, some people have been actively hurt by religion. If you experienced some form of abuse as a result of religion, please describe that here, as well as what sort of healing you have had from that experience.

If you experienced abuse as a result of religion and you have had no healing from that experience, what can you do now to heal that injury so that you can more easily explore this aspect of wellbeing?

Spiritual practice set apart from a religion requires you to develop your own "church," with your own routine of meditation, prayer, ceremony or whatever you deem to be a regular part of your day/week. If this is your intention, please write your ideas about how you will develop a daily/weekly spiritual practice that is an embedded practice to develop your inner life.

Religions and spiritual practices are culturally and developmentally diverse in faith, morality, values, ego, worldview, institutions and more, with far reaching implications on values, behaviors and relationships. For many, spirituality takes the form of religious observance, prayer, meditation or a belief in a higher power. For others, it can be found in nature, music, art or a secular community. Spirituality is different for everyone. Watch out though. When guilt, sin, shame and punishment are core themes, the health benefits are not realized. Positive thoughts bring positive practices, which bring positive habits.

Your deeply held beliefs strongly influence your health. So, take some time now to write about your religious or spiritual beliefs. Touch on what is most meaningful to you in this regard.

Chapter 8 | Spirituality

In the space below, use colored pencils or crayons to draw a picture of your concept of a Higher Power. Or, cut out pictures or words from magazines to place here to illustrate your Higher Power.

Possible Actions for Implementation

To foster spirituality in your lifestyle, examine your own values. Ask yourself:

1. What defines me as a person?
2. What role has religion or spirituality played in my life?
3. What is important to me?
4. How well do my daily activities reflect my values?
5. Do I neglect issues that matter to me because I'm busy spending time on things that matter less?
6. What are my important relationships?
7. What people give me a sense of community?
8. What/who inspires me and gives me hope?
9. What brings me joy?
10. What are my proudest achievements?

In the pages that follow, write about your answers to these questions. Take your time, as this is important.

Chapter 8 | Spirituality

Chapter 8 | Spirituality

Every one of the other seven Therapeutic Lifestyle Changes has an aspect of spiritual practice in it. Establishing healthy, loving relationships, spending time in and preserving the beauty of nature, conscious, sustainable eating, caring for the body through exercise and relaxation, enjoying laughter and fun, and doing for others all have spiritual components. Remembering the hopes and dreams you had before addiction sidetracked you from your true self is part of your journey.

Forgiveness —including the willingness to forgive oneself and others—will make you less angry, more hopeful, and better able to deal with emotions. Forgiveness reduces the build up of stress hormones that accompany negative emotions like anger and resentment and help you maintain homeostasis. Who are the people in your life that you need to forgive? (Please don't confuse forgiveness with having to let destructive people back into your life. It simply means that you have let go of thoughts of resentment and revenge.)

The power of prayer is widely practiced across all cultures. The act of putting oneself in the presence of your Higher Power is an important part of daily life. Prayer and meditation are particularly helpful tools for recovery and abstinence from addictive behaviors. When praying for yourself or others, an easy prayer goes like this:

May I be happy. May I be free from pain. May I be free. May I have all that I need to live my highest and best life. And, *May _____ be happy. May _____ be free from pain. May _____ be free. May _____ have all that he/she needs to live his/her highest and best life.*

You can, of course, pray the prayers of your religious faith, and you can make up your own. Use this space to write your own prayer.

This search for meaning can be conducted on your own as well as part of a larger religious community, with friends, in therapy or through your family. But, a simple affirmation of your life's purpose could be, *"May I be the one to break the dysfunctional patterns of my lineage, and may I bring forward the good, the true and the beautiful from my lineage."*

What would you like to say about your current understanding of your life's purpose … the reason you came here to planet Earth, and what you are meant to do with your life?

Do you have spiritual beliefs, worries or concerns that are causing you stress? If so, please write about them here. These should be discussed with your group leader, therapist or a spiritual adviser.

Affirmations are a wonderful way to enhance your spiritual life. An affirmation is a positive statement made to draw positive energy into your thoughts and beliefs about yourself, and your place in the world. When you have intention, fueled by affirmations and a plan of action, you are creating a directional compass. Here are a few affirmations that I especially like. You can use them if you like them, and its good to create your own.

…..I am healthy in every possible way. I am physically healthy. I am mentally healthy. I am emotionally healthy. I am spiritually healthy. I am healthy in every possible way.

…..I am living my best life; striving for the highest and best use of my gifts and talents.

…..My relationships are loving and filled with kindness and respect.

…..Gratitude is the by word of my life.

Now that I've given you some examples, please write several of your own affirmations to be said daily.

_____

_____

_____

_____

_____

_____

_____

Remember that the sweet territory of silent meditation is a wonderful addition to anyone's spiritual practice. When the Catholic nun, Mother Teresa was asked, "When you pray, what do you say to God?" She replied, "I don't talk. I simply listen." The interviewer then asked, "Ah, then, what is it that God says to you when you pray?" She replied, "He also doesn't talk. He also listens."

Sitting silently for 5-15 minutes each day and simply basking in the silence can be quite refreshing. It can also be very hard for a beginner. But, please try it. And, stay with it, even though it can be challenging. You'll get better at it and will come to enjoy the peace that comes as a result.

Try sitting in silence for 10 minutes and write about your experience.

This chapter on spirituality would not be complete without the suggestion of a Gratitude Journal. Gratitude is a spiritual principle. Gratitude opens the heart and shifts the energy of challenging situations. I hope that you have a Gratitude Journal that you write in during your devotional time every day. Take pleasure in small things, like birds singing, as well as the larger WOW things in life. Make a note here about creating a Gratitude Journal if you don't already have one.

Your Ideas

Use this space to make a preliminary plan to make a religious or spiritual practice part of your everyday life. Comment on the time of day, what you will do, what supplies you might need, if others will be present or not and how long you will spend. Note which of the following possibilities you will include. Remember, this is a beginning plan, so make it doable for now and adjust it as time goes on.

- Attend faith-based service
- Meditate daily
- Practice Yoga
- Join a choir
- Surround myself with believers
- Gratitude Journal
- Read a daily devotional
- Read scripture daily
- Other

Your Ideas

Benefits of Spirituality

- Gratitude
- Positivity and optimism
- Development of Compassion
- Pro-social emotions develop
- Positive relationships
- A path to self-actualization
- Character development
- A pro-social moral code
- Comfort in times of trouble

Final Words

"Health is a state of complete physical, mental and social wellbeing, and not merely the absence of disease or infirmity."
—*World Health Organization*

As with so many things in life, including recovery from addiction, the solutions are simple, but not necessarily easy. If you are reading these words, you have an understanding of what it means to apply Therapeutic Lifestyle Changes, as they have been presented here, to your program of recovery to optimize your mental health.

Much is made (and rightly so) of restoring the body after the ravages of addiction and plotting a program of recovery. Obviously, the first step is to become substance free. But that is just the beginning. If these other means of restoration, as outlined in this workbook, are neglected, a higher rate of relapse can be expected. Or, the individual is substance free, but just not very happy or operating optimally due to post acute withdrawal. This may be partly due to the fact that the individual's **mental** health has not been fully restored. The *8 Ways to Wellbeing for Recovering People,* as outlined in this workbook is the roadmap to optimize your mental health.

"Rome was not built in a day," as they say, and you are not likely to master all of these *8 Ways* in a short period of time. But, if you will continue to use this workbook, taking inventory of your progress from time to time, as you live your life in recovery, your mental health will definitely improve and your ability to stay disciplined about taking care of yourself will gradually get more efficient. It is truly the work of a lifetime.

My friend, Vickie Stringer, who served seven years in a Federal Penitentiary for drug trafficking, told me that she prayed in prison every day. She even wrote letters to God, making promises that she intended to keep and did keep upon her release. She offered me this quote from Joel 2:25 in *The Bible* that is a promise that sustained her and which I now pass on to you.

> *"I will restore to you what the locusts have eaten."*

Addiction is definitely like locusts. It eats a wide swath through a person's life, leaving ruins. There is a promise of restoration if you can just start on the path that has been laid out here.

My wish for you is that you take the time to heal and progress in all of these 8 aspects of optimizing mental health, and that you are restored and continue restoring, so that you can enjoy your life to the fullest and be a blessing in the lives of others in your family and community, delivering your gifts and talents generously in only the ways that **you** can.

Good Luck!

References

Alexander, C. & Langer, E. (1990). *Higher stages of human development.* New York: Oxford University Press.

Alexander, C. N., Rainforth, M. V., & Gelderloos, P. (1991). Transcendental meditation, self-actualization, and psychological health: A conceptual overview and statistical meta-analysis. *Journal of Social Behavior and Personality, 6,* 189-247.

Amminger, G.P., Schäfer, M.R., Papageorgiou, K., Klier, C.M., Cotton, S., Harrigan, S.M., ... Berger, G.E. (2010). Long-chain ω-3 fatty acids for indicated prevention of psychotic disorders: A randomized, placebo-controlled trial. *Archives of General Psychiatry, 67(2),* 146-154.

Anderson, J., Liu, C. & Kryscio, R. (2008). Blood pressure response to transcendental meditation: A meta-analysis. *American Journal of Hypertension, 21,* 310-316.

Angell, M. (2009). Drug companies and doctors: A story of corruption. *The New York Review of Books, LVI (1),* 8, 10, 12.

Anthes, E. (2009). Building around the mind. *Scientific American Mind, 20,* 52-59.

Appleton, K., Rogers, P. & Ness, A. (2010). Updated systematic review and meta-analysis of the effects of n-3 long-chain polyunsaturated fatty acids on depressed mood. *American Journal of Clinical Nutrition, 91(3),* 757-770.

Arias, A. J., Steinberg, K., Banga, A., & Trestman, R. L. (2006). Systematic review of the efficacy of meditation techniques as treatments for medical illness. *The Journal of Alternative and Complementary Medicine, 12,* 817-832.

Barrett, W. (1962). *Irrational man: A study in existential philosophy.* New York, NY: Doubleday.

Berman, M., Jonides, J., & Kaplan, S. (2008). The cognitive benefits of interacting with nature. *Psychological Science, 19,* 1207-1212.

Bhandari, H. & Yasunobu, K. (2009). What is social capital? A comprehensive review of the concept. *Asian Journal of Social Science 37(3)*, 480-510.

Bjorklund, D. F. & Pellegrini, A. D. (2002). *The origins of human nature.* Washington DC: American Psychological Association.

Black, D. S., Milam, J., & Sussman, S. (2009). Sitting-meditation interventions among youth: A review of treatment efficacy. *Pediatrics, 124,* e532-e541.

Borgonovi, F. (2009). Doing well by doing good: The relationship between formal volunteering and self-reported happiness. *Social Science and Medicine, 66,* 2312-2334.

Brown, S., Nesse, R., Vinokur, A., & Smith, D. (2003). Providing social support may be more beneficial than receiving it. *Psychological Science, 14:* 320-327

Bracken, C., Skalski, P. (2010). Immersed in media: Telepresence in everyday life. New York: Routledge.

Buss, D. (2000). The evolution of happiness. *American psychologist, 55(1),* 15-23.

Cattaneo, L. & Rizzolatti, G. (2009). The mirror neuron system. *Archives of Neurology, 66(5),* 557-560.

Cherniak, E.P., Troen, B.R., Florez, H.J., Roos, B.A. & Levis, S. (2009). Some new food for thought: The role of vitamin D in the mental health of older adults. *Current Psychiatry Reports, 11(1),* 12-19. doi: 10.1007/s11920-009-0003-3

Chiesa, A. (2009). Zen meditation: An integration of current evidence. *Journal of Alternative and Complementary Medication, 15,* 585-592.

Chiesa, A. & Serretti, A. (2009) Mindfulness-based stress reduction for stress management in healthy people: A   review and meta-analysis. *The Journal of Alternative and Complementary Medicine. 15(5),* 593-600.   doi:10.1089/acm.2008.0495

Christakis, N.A. (2009). "You make me sick!" doi: 10.1136/bmj.b2739

Christofoletti, G., Oliani, M., Gobbi, S, & Stella, F. (2007). Effects of motor intervention in elderly patients with dementia: An analysis of randomized controlled trials. *Topics in Geriatric Rehabilitation, 23 (2),* 149-   154. doi: 10.1097/01.TGR.0000270183.90778.8e

Clark, C. & Stansfeld, S. (2007). The effect of transportation noise on health and cognitive development: A review of recent evidence. *International Journal of Comparative Psychology, (20),* 145-158.

Colcombe, S. & Kramer, A. F. (2003). Fitness effects on the cognitive function of older adults: A meta-analytic study. *Psychological Science, 14,* 125-130.

Cotman, C. & Berchtold, N. (2002). Exercise: A behavioral intervention to enhance brain health and plasticity. *Neuroscience, 25:* 295-301.

References

Cummins, R.A. (2005). The domains of life satisfaction: An attempt to order chaos. In A.C. Michalos (Ed.) *Citation Classics from Social Indicators Research*. (pp 559-584). Netherlands: Springer.

da Silva, T., Ravindran, L., & Ravindran, A. (2009). Yoga in the treatment of mood and anxiety disorders: A review. *Asian Journal of Psychiatry, 2,* 6-16.

Daley, A. J. (2002). Exercise therapy and mental health in clinical populations: Is exercise therapy a worthwhile intervention? *Advances in Psychiatric Treatment, 8:* 262-270.

Dawkins, R. (2006). *The God delusion.* Boston, MA: Houghton Mifflin.

Delpeuch, F., Marie, B., Monnnier, E., & Holdsworth, M. (2009). *Globesity: A planet out of control.* London: Earthscan Publications.

Deslandes, A., Moraes, H., Ferreira, C., Veiga, H., Silveria, H., Mouta, R., ...Laks, J. (2009). Exercise and mental health: Many reasons to move. *Neuropsychobiology, 59,* 191-198.

Devlin, A. & Arneill, A. (2003). Health care environments and patient outcomes: A review of the literature. *Environment and Behavior, 35,* 665.

Didonna, F. (Ed.). (2009). *Clinical handbook of mindfulness.* New York: Springer.

Dowd, S., Vickers, K., & Krahn, D. (2004). Exercise for depression. *Journal of Current Psychiatry, 3,* 10-20.

Duncan, B.L., Miller, S.O., Wampold, B.E. & Hubble, M.A. (Eds.). (2010). *The heart and soul of change: Delivering what works in therapy,* 2nd ed. Washington DC.: American Psychological Association.

Dunn, D., Aknin, L., & Norton, M. (2009). Spending money on others promotes happiness. *Science, 319,* 1687-1688.

Dusek, J., Otu, H., Wohlhueter, A., Zerbini, L., Joseph, M., Benson, H., ...Hasin, M. (2008). Genomic counter-stress changes induced by the relaxation response. *PLOS One, 3,* e2576.

Erikson, E. (1959). *Identity and the life cycle.* New York, NY: International University press.

Erikson, K. & Kramer, A. (2009). Aerobic exercise effects on cognitive and neural plasticity in older adults. *British Journal of Sports Medicine, 43,* 22-24.

Esbjorn-Hargens, S. & Zimmerman, M. (2009). *Integral ecology.* Boston: Integral Books.

Fischer, C. (2004). The 2004 GSS Finding of Shrunken Social Networks: An artifact? Published online by *American Sociological Review,* 74(4), 657-669. doi: 10.1177/000312240907400408

Fotuhi, M., Mohassel, P., & Yaffe, K. (2009). Fish consumption, long-chain omega-3 fatty acids and risk of cognitive decline or Alzheimer disease: A complex association. *Nature clinical practice.Neurology, 5,* 140-152.

Fowler, J. & Christakis, N. (2008). Dynamic spread of happiness in a large social network. *BMJ, 337:* a2338.

Fowler, J. & Christakis, N. (2010). Cooperative behavior cascades in human social networks. *Proceedings of the National Academy of Sciences, 107(12),* 5334-5338.

Fowler, J.W. (1995). *Stages of faith: The psychology of human development.* New York: HarperOne

Frattaroli, J., Weidner, G., Dnistrian, A., Kemp, C., Daubenmier, J., & Marlin, R. (2009). Clinical events in prostate cancer lifestyle trial: Results from two years of follow-up. *Urology, 72,* 1319-1323.

Fredrickson, B. (2002). Positive emotions. In C.Snyder & S. Lopez (Eds.), *Handbook of positive psychology* (pp. 120-134). New York, NY: Oxford University Press.

Freeman, M., Hibbeln, J., Wisner, K., Davis, J., Mischoulon, D., Peet, M., ...Stoll, A. (2006). Omega-3 fatty acids: Evidence basis for treatment and future research in psychiatry. *Journal of Clinical Psychiatry, 67,* 1954-1967.

Gebauer, J., Riketta, M., Broemer, P., & Mai, G. (2008). Pleasure and pressure based prosocial motivation: Divergent relations to subjective well-being. *Journal of Research in Personality, 42,* 399-420.

Gillies, P. (2007). Preemptive nutrition of pro-inflammatory states: A nutrigenomic model. *Nutritional Reviews, 65,* S217-S220.

Gomez-Pinilla, J. (2008). Brainfoods: The effect of nutrients on brain function. *Nature Reviews Neuroscience, 9,* 568-578.

Gopnik, A. (2008). Right again: The passions of John Stuart Mill. *The New Yorker,* October, 6, 85-91.

Gordon, D. (1999). The Epicurean option. *Philosophy Now, 24,* 33-35.

Gordon, G. & Esbjorn-Hargens, S. (2007). Integral play. *Journal of Integral Theory and Practice, 2,* 62-104.

Grimm, R., Spring, K., & Dietz, N. (2007). *The health benefits of volunteering: A review of recent research.* Washington, D.C.: Corporation for National and Community Service.

Gu, Y., Nieves, J.W., Stern, Y., Luchsinger, J.A. & Scarmeas, N. (2010). *Archives of Neurology, 67(6).* doi: 10.1001/archneurol.2010.84

Hamer, M. & Chida, Y. (2009). Physical activity and risk of neurodegenerative disease: a systematic review of prospective evidence. *Psychological Medicine, 39,* 3-11.

Hamer, M. & Chida, Y. (2008). Exercise and depression: A meta-analysis and critical review. In W.Hansson & E. Olsson (Eds.). *New perspectives on women and depression* (pp. 255-266). New York: Nova Science Publishers Inc.

Harris, S. (2005). *The End of Faith*. New York, NY: W.W. Norton.

Hertzog, C., Kramer, A., Wilson, R., & Lindenberger, U. (2009). Fit body, fit mind? *Scientific American Mind, 20,* 24-31.

Higgins, S., Hall, E., Wall, K., Woolner, P., & McCaughey, C. (2005). The impact of school environments: A literature review. http://www.cfbt.com/PDF/91085.pdf

Hitchens, C. (2007). *God is not great*. New York, NY: Twelve Books.

Ho, C., Payne, L., Orsega-Smith, E., & Godby, G. (2003). Parks, recreation, and public health. *Parks & Recreation, 38,* 18, 20-27.

Hoffman, S.G., Sawyer, A.T., Witt, A.A. & Oh, D. (2010). The effect of mindfulness-based therapy on anxiety and depression: A meta-analytic review. *Journal of Consulting Clinical Psychology, 78(2),* 169-183. doi: 10.1037/a0018555

Hopkins, J. (2001). *Cultivating compassion*. New York, NY: Broadway Books.

Innis, S. M. (2009). Omega-3 fatty acids and neural development to two years of age. *Journal of Pediatric Gastroenterology and Nutrition, 48,* S16-S24.

Ito, M., Horst, H., Brittani, M., Boyd, D., Herr-Stephenson, B., Lang, P., ...Robinson, L. (2008). *Living and learning with new media: Summary of findings from the digital youth project*. Cambridge: The MIT Press.

Jetten, J., Haslam, C., Haslam, S., & Branscombe, N. (2009). The social cure. *Scientific American Mind, 20,* 26-33.

Kang, J. H., Ascherio, A., & Groodstein, F. (2005). Fruit and vegetable consumption and cognitive decline in aging women. *Annals of Neurology, 57,* 713-720.

Kessler, D. (2009). *The end of overeating*. New York, NY: Rodale Press.

Khaw, K. T., Wareham, N., Bingham, S., Welch, A., & Luben, R. (2008). Combined impact of health behaviors and mortality in men and women. *Obstetrical & Gynecological Survey, 63,* 376-377.

Kirkwood, G., Rampes, H., Tuffrey, V., Richardson, J., & Pilkington, K. (2005). Yoga for anxiety: A systematic review of the research evidence. *British Journal of Sports Medicine, 39,* 884-891.

Koenig, H. (2002). *Spirituality in patient care*. Philadelphia, PA: Templeton Foundation Press.

Koenig, H. G. (2009). Research on religion, spirituality, and mental health: A review. *Canadian Journal of Psychiatry, 54,* 283-291.

Koenig, H. G., McCullough, M. E., & Larson, D. B. (2001). *Handbook of religion and health*. Oxford University Press.

Kraguljac, N.V., Montori, V.M., Pavuluri, M., Chai, H.S., Wilson, B.S. & Unal, S.S. (2009). Efficacy of omega-3 fatty acids in mood disorders - a systematic review and metaanalysis. *Psychopharmaology Bulletin, 42(3)*, 39-54.

Kuller, R., Ballal, S., Laike, T., Mikellides, B., & Tonello, G. (2006). The impact of light and colour on psychological mood: A cross-cultural study of indoor work environments. *Ergonomics, 49*, 1496-1507.

Kuramoto, A. (2006). Therapeutic benefits of Tai Chi exercise: Research review. *Wisconsin Medical Journal, 105*, 42-46.

Langerok, H. (1915). A study of professional deformation. *The American Journal of Sociology, 21*, 30-34.

Larun, L., Nordeim, L., Ekeland, E., Hagen, K., & Heian, F. (2006). Exercise in prevention and treatment of anxiety and depression among children and young people. *Cochrane Database of Systematic Reviews.* http://www2.cochrane.org/reviews/en/ab004691.html

Lester, S. & Russell, W. (2008). *Play for a change - play, policy and practice: A review of contemporary perspectives.* London: National Children's Bureau.

Lefcourt, H. (2002). Humor. In C.Snyder & S. Lopez (Eds.), *Handbook of positive psychology* (pp. 619-631). New York, NY: Oxford University Press.

Lin, P. & Su, K. (2007). A meta-analytic review of double-blind, placebo-controlled trials of antidepressant efficacy of omega-3 fatty acids. *Journal of Clinical Psychiatry, 68*, 1056-1061.

Lipton, L. (2008). Using yoga to treat disease: An evidence based review. *Journal of the American Academy of Physician Assistants, 21*, 34, 36, 38, 41.

Long, B. J., Calfas, K. J., Wooten, W., Sallis, J. F., Patrick, K., Goldstein, M., ...Heath, G.. (1996). A multisite field test of the acceptability of physical activity counseling in primary care: Project PACE. *American Journal of Preventative Medicine, 12*, 73-81.

Louve, R. (2005). *Last child in the woods: Saving our children from nature-deficit disorder.* Chapel Hill, NC: Algonquin Books of Chapel Hill.

Luhrmann, T. M. (2001). *Of two minds: An anthropologist looks at American psychiatry.* New York, NY: Vintage.

Maller, C., Townsend, M., Pryor, A., Brown, P., & Sleger, L. (2006). Healthy nature, healthy people: 'Contact with nature' as an upstream health promotion intervention for populations. *Health Promotion International, 21*, 45-54.

Manzoni, G. M., Pagnini, F., Castelnuovo, G., & Molinari, E. (2008). Relaxation training for anxiety: a ten-year sytematic review with meta-analysis. *BMC Psychiatry, 8*, 1-12.

Mares, M.L. & Woodard, E. (2005). Positive effects of television on children's social interactions: A meta-analysis. *MediaPsychology, 7(3),* 301-322.

McEntee, D. & Halgin, R. (1996). Therapists' attitudes about addressing the role of exercise in psychotherapy. *Journal of Clinical Psychology, 52,* 48-60.

McMorris, T., Tomporowski, P. & Audiffren, M. (2009). *Exercise and cognitive function.* Chichester, England: Wiley-Blackwell

McPherson, M., Smith-Lovin, L. & Brashears, M.E. (2006). Social isolation in America: Changes in core discussion networks over two decades. *American Sociological Review, 71(3),* 353-375. doi: 10.1177/000312240607100301

Mojtabai, R. & Olfson, M. (2008). National trends in psychotherapy by office-based psychiatrists. *Archives of General Psychiatry, 65,* 962-970.

Montanye, J. A. (2001). Bowling alone: The collapse and revival of an American community. *The Independent Review, 5(3).* http://www.independent.org/publications/tir/article.asp?a=205

Morris, M., Evans, D., Tangney, C., Bienias, J., & Wilson, R. (2006). Associations of vegetable and fruit consumption with age-related cognitive change. *Neurology, 67:* 1370-1376.

Noaghuil, S. & Hibbeln, J. (2003). Cross-national comparisons of seafood consumption and rates of bipolar disorder. *American Journal of Psychiatry, 160,* 2222-2227.

Norcross, J. (2010). The therapeutic relationship. In B. Duncan, S. Miller, B. Wampold, M. Hubble, M. (Eds.). *The heart and soul of change: Delivering what works in therapy,* 2nd *ed.* (pp. 113-142).Washington, DC: American Psychological Association.

Oken, E., Radesky, J. S., Wright, R. O., Bellinger, D. C. & Chitra, J., Amarasiriwardena, ... Gillman, M.W. (2008). Maternal fish intake during pregnancy, blood mercury levels, and child cognition at age 3 years in a U.S. cohort. *American Journal of Epidemiology, 167,* 1171-1181.

Ornish, D., Lin, J., Daubenmier, J., Weidner, G., Epel, E., Kemp, C., ...Carroll, P. (2008). Increased telomerase activity and comprehensive lifestyle changes: A pilot study. *The Lancet Oncology, 9,* 1048-1057.

Ospina, M. B., Bond, T. K., Karkhaneh, M., Tjosvold, L., Vandermeer, B. & Liang, Y....Klassen, T.P. (2007). *Meditation practices for health: State of the research.* AHRQ Publication No.07-E010. http://www.ahrq.gov/downloads/pub/evidence/pdf/meditation/medit.pdf

Pagnoni, G. & Cekic, M. (2007). Age effects on gray matter volume and attentional performance in Zen meditation. *Neurobiological Aging, 28,* 1623-627.

Pilgrim, D., Rogers, A., & Bentall, R. (2009). The centrality of personal relationships in the creation and amelioration of mental health problems: The current interdisciplinary case. *Health: An interdisciplinary Journal for the Social Study of Health, Illness & Medicine, 13,* 235.

Pilkington, K., Kirkwood, G., Rampes, H., & Richardson, J. (2005). Yoga for depression: The research evidence. *Journal of Affective Disorders, 89,* 13-24.

Pischke, C.R., Scherwitz, L.,Weidner, G. & Ornish, D. (2008). Long-term effects of lifestyle changes on well-being and cardiac variables among coronary heart disease patients. *Health psychology, 27(5),* 584-592. doi: 10.1037/0278-6133.27.5.584

Post, S. (2007). *The science of altruism and health.* New York: Oxford Press.

Post, S. & Niemark, J. (2007). *Why good things happen to good people.* New York: Broadway Books.

Post, S., Underwood, L., Schloss, J., & Hulbert, W. (2002). *Altruism and altruistic love: Science, philosophy and religion in dialogue.* Oxford: Oxford University Press.

Preiss, R.W., Gayle, B.M., Burrell, N., Allen, M. & Bryant, J. (2006). *Mass media effects research: Advances through meta-analysis.* New York: Routledge Press.

Prolla, T. A. & Mattson, M. P. (2001). Molecular mechanisms of brain aging and neurodegenerative disorders: Lessons from dietary restriction. *Trends in Neurosciences, 24,* s21-s31.

Pryor, A., Townsend, M., Maller, C., & Field, K. (2006). Health and well-being naturally: 'Contact with nature' in health promotion for targeted individuals, communities and populations. *Health Promotion Journal of Australia, 17,* 114-223.

Putnam, R. D. (1995). Bowling alone: America's declining social capital. *Journal of Democracy, 6,* 65-78.

Putnam, R. D. (2000). *Bowling alone: The collapse and revival of American community.* New York: Simon Schuster.

Quaney, B.M., Boyd, L.A., McDown, J.M., Zahner, L.H., Jianghua, He, Mayo, M.S. & Macko, R.F. (2009). Aerobic exercise improves cognition and motor function poststroke. Neurorehabilitation and Neural Repair, 23(9), 879-885. doi: 10.1177/1545968309338193

Raji, C., Ho, A., Neelroop, P., Becker, J., Lopez, O., & Kuller, L. (2009). Brain structure and obesity. *Neuroimage, 47, (Supplement 1),* S39-S41.

Rusbult, C, Finkel, E. & Kumashiro, M. The Michelangelo phenomenon. *Current Directions in Psychological Science, 18(6),* 305-309.

Sarris, J., Schoendorfer, N., & Kavanagh, D. J. (2009). Major depressive disorder and nutritional medicine. *Nutrition Reviews, 67,* 125-131.

Shapiro, S. & Carlson, L. (2009). *The art and science of mindfulness.* Washington D.C.: American Psychological Association Press.

References

Shedler, J.K. (2010). "The efficacy of psychodynamic psychotherapy." *American Psychologist, 65(2)*, 98-109.

Sidhu, K., Vandana, P., & Balon, R. (2009). Exercise prescription: A practical effective therapy for depression. *Current Psychiatry, 8*, 39-51.

Small, G. & Vorgan, G. (2008). Meet your ibrain. *Scientific American Mind, 19*, 42-49.

Smith, E. (2000). *The body in psychotherapy*. Jefferson, N.C.: McFarland & Company.

Sofi, F., Cesari, F., Abbate, R., Gensini, G.F. & Casini, A. (2008). Adherence to Mediterranean diet and health status: meta-analysis. doi: 10.1136/bmj.a1344

Song, C. & Zhao, S. (2008). Omega-3 fatty acid eicosapentaenoic acid: A new treatment for psychiatric and neurodegenerative diseases. *Expert Opinion on Investigational Drugs, 16*, 1627-1638.

Stahl, L., Begg, D., Weisinger, R., & Sinclair, A. (2008). The role of omega-3 fatty acids in mood disorders. *Current Opinion in Investigational Drugs, 9*, 57-64.

Stathopoulou, G., Powers, M., Berry, A., Smits, J., & Otto, M. (2006). Exercise interventions for mental health: A quantitative and qualitative review. *Clinical Psychology: Science and Practice, 13*, 179-193.

Stranahan, A.M., Khalil, D. & Gould, E. (2006). Social isolation delays the positive effects of running on adult neurogenesis. *Nature Neuroscience, 9*, 526-533. doi: 10.1038/nn1668

Sui, X., Laditka, J., Church, T., Hardin, J., Chase, N., Davis, K. & Blair, S. (2009). Prospective study of cardiorespiratory fitness and depressive symptoms in women and men. *Journal of Psychiatric Research, 43*, 546-552.

Taylor, A. F. & Kuo, F. E. (2009). Children with attention deficits concentrate better after walk in the park. *Journal of Attention Disorders, 12*, 402-409.

Taylor, A. F., Kuo, F. E., & Sullivan, W. C. (2001). Coping with ADD: The surprising connection to green play settings. *Environment and Behavior, 33*, 54-77.

Thoreau, H. (1854). *Walden; or life in the woods*. Boston, MA: Ticknor & Fields.

Thoreau, H. (1921). *A week on the Concord and Merimack Rivers*. New York: Charles Scribner & Sons.

Tiffin, J. & Terashima, N. (2001). *HyperReality: Paradigm for the third millennium*. New York, NY: Routledge.

Trakhtenberg, E. (2008). The effects of guided imagery on the immune system: A critical review. *International Journal of Neuroscience, 118*, 839-855.

Ulrich, R. (2006). Evidence-based health care architecture. *The Lancet, 368:* 538-539.

Voren, R. V. (2002). Comparing Soviet and Chinese political psychiatry. *Journal of the American Academy of Psychiatry and the Law, 30*, 131-135.

Walsh, R. (1999). *Essential spirituality: The seven central practices*. New York: Wiley & Sons.

Walsh, R. The state of the integral enterprise, Part I: Current status, possible applications, and potential traps. *Journal of Integral Theory and Practice*, 4(3), 1-12, 2009.

Walsh, R. Contemplative psychotherapies. In R. Corsini & Wedding (Eds.) *Current psychotherapies (9th ed.)*. Belmont, CA: Thomson, in press.

Walsh, R. & Shapiro, S. (2006). The meeting of meditative disciplines and Western psychology: A mutually enriching dialogue. *American Psychologist, 61*, 227-239.

Wang, W., Zhang, A., Rasmussen, B., Lin, L., Dunning, T., Kang, S., ...Lo, S.K. (2009). The effect of Tai chi on psychosocial well-being: A systematic review of randomized controlled trials. *Journal of Acupuncture and Meridian Studies, 2,* 171-181.

Wehrenberg, M. & Coppersmith, L. (2008). Technotrap: When work becomes your second home. *Psychotherapy Networker, 32(2),* 40-45,64.

WHO (2008). Controlling the global obesity epidemic. http://www.who.int/nutrition/topics/obesity/en/index.html

Wilber, K. (2000). *Integral psychology*. Boston: Shambhala.

Wilber, K. (2005). *A sociable God*. Boston: Shambhala.

Wilber, K. (2006). *Integral spirituality*. Boston: Shambhala.

Willis, L. M., Shukitt-Hale, B., & Joseph, J. A. (2009). Recent advances in berry supplementation and age related cognitive decline. *Current Opinion in Clinical Nutrition & Metabolic Care, 12,* 91-94.

Wolf, P., Beiser, A., Elias, M., Au, R., Vasan, R., & Seshradi, S. (2007). Relations to obesity in cognitive function: The Framingham heart study. *Current Alzheimer Research, 4,* 111-116.

Wordsworth.W. (1998). *The collected poems of William Wordsworth*. Hertfordshire, Great Britain: Wordsworth Editions Ltd.

Xiong, G. L. & Doraiswamy, P. M. (2009). Does meditation enhance cognition and brain plasticity? *Annals of the New York Academy of Sciences, 1172,* 63-69.

Yalom, I. (2002). *The gift of therapy*. New York: Harper Collins.

About the Author

Dr. Sonnee Weedn is a clinical and forensic psychologist with offices in Novato and Newport Beach, CA. She is a Certified Sex Addiction Therapist and an APA certified specialist in the treatment of alcoholism and other chemical dependencies. She is certified to practice EMDR and Emotional Transformation Therapy, and began her practice in 1980 when Viet Nam veterans were beginning to manifest symptoms of trauma and substance abuse. It is with them that she learned to treat the dual diagnosis of PTSD and chemical dependency. She has performed evaluations through the Veteran's Administration for veterans seeking disability evaluations for mental health issues. Dr. Weedn has been in private practice since 1980, treating individuals, couples, and families, as well as maintaining three long-term therapy groups, and coaching executives and athletes.

She is the founder of the Sonnee Weedn Institute for Integrative Therapies, which has provided funding for various educational enterprises, especially those that emphasize cross-cultural bridgework, including: African American history in story and song, with Dr. Ysaye Barnwell, founding member of the a capella group, Sweet Honey in the Rock; trainings with Native Americans, Albert Sombrero (Navajo) and Lench Archuleta (Yaqui); and Tibetan Buddhist monk and humanitarian, Lama Tenzin Choegyal and with The Medium of the State Oracle of Tibet, Ven. Thupten Ngodup. Her Institute donated $52,000 to the Tibetan Medical and Astrological Society and Tibetan Children's Villages in 2014.

Dr. Weedn has conducted trainings in: group psychotherapy as transformational experience; spirituality for recovering people; treatment for psychological trauma; psychosynthesis for the contemporary therapist; the use of NeuroCodex® and NeuroCoach® for diagnosis and treatment of addiction, concussion and other brain-based issues; and psychological testing for non-psychologists, including events in Puerto Vallarta, Mexico, Delhi, Dharmsala, and Rishikesh, India, and various venues in the United States.

In October 2015 and 2016, she was an invited speaker for His Holiness, the 14th Dalai Lama's *Mind, Body, Life Conference* (Men-Tsee Khang) in Dharmsala, India.

She consults to various treatment organizations in the area of continuing education for mental health professionals, and program development and implementation. Her consulting includes Elements Behavioral Health Promises, The Meadows, The Refuge, IITAP, Windward Way, Casa Capri the Ben Franklin Institute, Sierra Tucson, and The Heart Reconnection Institute.

NASA astronaut, Col. (ret.) Yvonne Cagle, M.D., invited Dr. Weedn to be a founding member and chairman of the DSR-30 (Deep Space Research – 2030) Consortium, writing behavioral health protocols maintenance and monitoring of behavioral health for the astronauts going to Mars in the future. This consortium combines the talents of members from Fordham University and researchers, physicians and psychologists from varying areas of behavioral health.

Her interest in ethnopsychology has inspired her to study with spiritual leaders of various ethnicities and wisdom traditions, including Navajo Roadman, Albert Sombrero; Yaqui Spirit Guide, Lorenzo Archuleta, Presbyterian pastor, Rev. George McLaird, Tibetan Buddhist monk, Lama Tenzin Choegyal, Hindu Swami, Sri Sri Ganapathi Sachchodananda, and cultural anthropologist, Angeles Arrien, Ph.D., among others.

She is an award-winning author of the book, *Many Blessings: A Tapestry of Accomplished African American Women,* in which she interviewed and wrote the life stories of 30 resilient and resourceful contemporary African American women including: the former U.S. Surgeon General, Dr. Joycelyn Elders; actress Loretta Devine; Cheryl Boone-Issacs, President of the Academy of Motion Pictures; Col. Yvonne Cagle, M.D., NASA astronaut; Fulbright scholar, Dr. Valata Jenkins-Monroe, to name a few.

In addition, she won the Clark Vincent Award, along with Alexandra Katehakis, MFT and Jill Vermiere, MFT, given by the California Association of Marriage and Family Therapists for her contributions to two chapters (group psychotherapy and diagnosis) in the textbook, *Making Advances: A Comprehensive Treatment Guide for Female Sex and Love Addicts.*

About the Author

Most recently, she has begun working with neuro-engineer Dr. Curtis Cripe repairing the neurological/cognitive damage done to the brain due to substance abuse or head trauma. Neuro-engineering can improve or eliminate the symptoms of depression, anxiety, bipolar neuro, learning disabilities, attention problems, and people on the autism spectrum, among other psychiatric problems.

She maintains priviliges at Hoag Hospital Newport Beach.

Dr. Weedn considers her greatest accomplishments to be her marriage of 50 years to Robert Weedn, and her adult sons, Isaiah and Simon. She is grandmother to Daylan and Parker Sonnee.

APPENDIX A
Worksheets

Life Assessment

NAME_____ DATE_____

Healthy habits can give you the life you want. As you work on building a healthy future for yourself, periodically take a moment to assess what you like and dislike about all areas of your life. Rate each on a 1-5 scale, with 5 being most satisfied and 1 indicating a lot of improvement is needed. Begin making changes in the lowest scored areas and set goals and action plan to work on.

1. Health & Wellness   _____

2. Lifestyle & Fun   _____

3. Career & Work   _____

4. Family & Friends   _____

5. Love & Romance   _____

6. Money & Finances   _____

7. Personal Growth & Education   _____

8. Spirituality   _____

Support Group

NAME _____ DATE _____

Today	In The Future
PROFESSIONALS (therapist, psychiatrist, lawyer. Physician, trainer, job counselor, spiritual advisor) 1. _____ 2. _____ 3. _____ 4. _____	**PROFESSIONALS** (job counselor, therapist, psychiatrist lawyer, physician, trainer, spiritual advisor) 1. _____ 2. _____ 3. _____ 4. _____
FAMILY (spouse/partner, parent, sibling, relative) 1. _____ 2. _____ 3. _____ 4. _____	**FAMILY** (spouse/partner, parent, sibling, relative) 1. _____ 2. _____ 3. _____ 4. _____
FRIENDS 1. _____ 2. _____ 3. _____ 4. _____	**FRIENDS** 1. _____ 2. _____ 3. _____ 4. _____
OTHER SUPPORT (teacher, neighbor, 12-step group, sponsor, religious leader, advisor) 1. _____ 2. _____ 3. _____ 4. _____	**OTHER SUPPORT** (teacher, neighbor, 12-step group, sponsor, religious leader, advisor) 1. _____ 2. _____ 3. _____ 4. _____
PETS 1. _____ 2. _____ 3. _____ 4. _____	**PETS** 1. _____ 2. _____ 3. _____ 4. _____

Stressor Worksheet

NAME_____ DATE_____

- List the triggers that make you uncomfortable, reduce your functioning, and/or cause you to be tempted to relapse or act out in some way that is destructive to you or others.

- Write down the people, situations, times, places and/or events that trigger unhealthy thoughts and behaviors.

- Then, write down how you plan to respond differently with healthy thinking and activities.

WHO	
WHAT	
WHERE	
WHEN	
WHY	
-HOW-	
WHO	
WHAT	
WHERE	
WHEN	
WHY	
-HOW-	
WHO	
WHAT	
WHERE	
WHEN	
WHY	
-HOW-	

ns
Stressor Worksheet

NAME_____ DATE_____

- List the triggers that make you uncomfortable, reduce your functioning, and/or cause you to be tempted to relapse or behave in ways you regret.

- Write down the people, situations, times, places and/or events that trigger unhealthy thoughts and behaviors.

- Then, write down how you plan to respond differently with healthy thinking and activities.

Progress Charts & Journal

CALL TO ACTION

Today, I will _____

_____

This week, I will _____

_____

This month, I will _____

_____

Habit Change Worksheet

TRIGGER	ROUTINE ACTION	REWARD

TRIGGER Identification

Item	Day 1	Day 2	Day 3
Where Are You?			
What Time Is It?			
Your Emotional State?			
Who Else Is Around?			
What Action Preceded?			

Weekly Action Plan

This week, I will take care of my body by: _____

_____

_____

This week, I will take care of my mind by: _____

_____

_____

This week, I will take care of my spirit by: _____

_____

_____

This week, I will take care of my relationships by: _____

_____

_____

This week, I will take care of my environment by: _____

_____

_____

This week, I will take care of my appearance by: _____

_____

_____

Nutrition Goal Setting Worksheet

NAME_____ DATE_____

My Nutrition Goal is: _____

_____

_____

_____

Goal Completion Date: _____

I will know I have reached my goal because: _____

_____

_____

_____

Three things that will help me reach my goal:

1 _____

2 _____

3 _____

Two people who can help me reach my goal:

1 _____

2 _____

Steps to reaching my goal: _____

_____

_____

_____

_____

_____

Food Journal

NAME_____ WEEK_____

MEAL/SNACK	TIME	FOOD	BEVERAGE
Breakfast			
Morning Snack			
Lunch			
Afternoon Snack			
Dinner			
Evening Snack			

Appendix A | Worksheets

Nutrition Facts Label

What's On The Nutrition Facts Label

The Nutrition Facts Label found on packaged foods and beverages is your daily tool for making informed food choices that contribute to healthy lifelong eating habits. Explore it today and discover the wealth of information it contains!

Serving Size

Serving Size is based on the **amount of food that is customarily eaten** at one time. All of the nutrition information listed on the Nutrition Facts Label is based on **one serving** of the food.

The serving size is shown as a common household measure that is appropriate to the food (such as cup, tablespoon, piece, slice, or jar), followed by the metric amount in grams (g).

When comparing calories and nutrients in different foods, check the serving size in order to make an accurate comparison.

Servings Per Container

Servings Per Container shows the **total number of servings** in the entire food package or container. It is common for one package of food to contain more than one serving.

The information listed on the Nutrition Facts Label is based on **one serving**. So, if a package contains *two servings* and you eat the entire package, you have consumed *twice the amount of calories and nutrients* listed on the label.

Calories

Calories refers to the **total number of calories**, or "energy," supplied from all sources (fat, carbohydrate, protein, and alcohol) in one serving of the food.

To achieve or maintain a healthy body weight, balance the number of calories you eat and drink with the number of calories you burn during physical activity and through your body's metabolic processes.

> As a general rule:
> **100 calories** per serving is **moderate**
> **400 calories** per serving is **high**

Nutrition Facts	
Serving Size 1 package (272g)	
Servings Per Container 1	
Amount Per Serving	
Calories 300	Calories from Fat 45
	% Daily Value*
Total Fat 5g	8%
Saturated Fat 1.5g	8%
Trans Fat 0g	
Cholesterol 30mg	10%
Sodium 430mg	18%
Total Carbohydrate 55g	18%
Dietary Fiber 6g	24%
Sugars 23g	
Protein 14g	
Vitamin A	80%
Vitamin C	35%
Calcium	6%
Iron	15%

* Percent Daily Values are based on a 2,000 calorie diet. Your Daily Values may be higher or lower depending on your calorie needs:

		Calories:	2,000	2,500
Total Fat		Less than	65g	80g
Saturated Fat		Less than	20g	25g
Cholesterol		Less than	300mg	300mg
Sodium		Less than	2,400mg	2,400mg
Total Carbohydrate			300g	375g
Dietary Fiber			25g	30g

> **Tip:** "Fat-free" doesn't mean "calorie-free." Some lower fat food items may have as many calories as the full-fat version. Always check the Nutrition Facts Label and compare the calories and nutrients in the fat-free version to the regular version.

Calories from Fat

Calories from Fat are *not* additional calories, but are **fat's contribution to the total number of calories** in one serving of the food. The Nutrition Facts Label lists the calories from fat because fat has more than *twice* the number of calories per gram than carbohydrate or protein.

For example, if the Nutrition Facts Label says one serving of food contains 150 calories and 100 calories from fat, the remaining 50 calories comes from carbohydrate, protein, and/or alcohol.

What's On The Nutrition Facts Label 1

Percent Daily Value (%DV)

Percent Daily Value (%DV) shows **how much of a nutrient is in one serving** of the food. The %DVs are based on the Daily Values for key nutrients, which are the amounts (in grams, milligrams, or micrograms) of nutrients recommended per day for Americans 4 years of age and older. The %DV column doesn't add up vertically to 100%. Instead, the %DV is the percentage of the Daily Value for each nutrient in one serving of the food.

For example, the Daily Value for saturated fat is 20 grams (g), which equals 100% DV. If the Nutrition Facts Label says one serving of a food contains 1.5 g of saturated fat, then the %DV for saturated fat for this specific food is 8%. That means the food contains 8% of the maximum amount of saturated fat that an average person should eat in an entire day.

Using the %DV

Compare Foods: Use the %DV to compare food products (remember to make sure the serving size is the same) and to choose products that are higher in nutrients you want to get more of and lower in nutrients you want to get less of.

> As a general rule:
> **5% DV** or less of a nutrient per serving is **low**
> **20% DV** or more of a nutrient per serving is **high**

Understand Nutrient Content Claims: Use the %DV to help distinguish one claim from another, such as "light," "low," and "reduced." Simply compare the %DVs in each food product to see which one is higher or lower in a particular nutrient; there is no need to memorize definitions.

Manage "Dietary Trade-Offs": Use the %DV to make dietary trade-offs with other foods throughout the day. You don't have to give up a favorite food to eat a healthy diet. When a food you like is high in a nutrient you want to get less of – or low in a nutrient you want to get more of – balance it with foods that are low (or high) in that nutrient at other times of the day.

Nutrition Facts

Serving Size 1 package (272g)
Servings Per Container 1

Amount Per Serving

Calories 300 — Calories from Fat 45

	% Daily Value*
Total Fat 5g	8%
Saturated Fat 1.5g	8%
Trans Fat 0g	
Cholesterol 30mg	10%
Sodium 430mg	18%
Total Carbohydrate 55g	18%
Dietary Fiber 6g	24%
Sugars 23g	
Protein 14g	
Vitamin A	80%
Vitamin C	35%
Calcium	6%
Iron	15%

* Percent Daily Values are based on a 2,000 calorie diet. Your Daily Values may be higher or lower depending on your calorie needs:

		Calories:	2,000	2,500
Total Fat		Less than	65g	80g
Saturated Fat		Less than	20g	25g
Cholesterol		Less than	300mg	300mg
Sodium		Less than	2,400mg	2,400mg
Total Carbohydrate			300g	375g
Dietary Fiber			25g	30g

Footnote

The Asterisk

The asterisk (*) following the heading "% Daily Value" on the Nutrition Facts Label refers to the standard footnote at the bottom of all labels, which specifies that some of the %DVs are based on a **2,000 calorie daily diet**. A 2,000 calorie daily diet is often used as the basis for general nutrition advice; however, your Daily Values may be higher or lower depending on your calorie needs. Calorie needs vary according to age, gender, height, weight, and physical activity level. Check your calorie needs at http://www.choosemyplate.gov.

Daily Value Recommendations

If there is enough space available on the food package, the footnote on the Nutrition Facts Label will also list the **Daily Values** for some key nutrients. These are given for both a 2,000 and 2,500 calorie daily diet. This section also includes **goals** regarding how much or how little of a nutrient to aim for in your daily diet. The Daily Values for some nutrients are different for a 2,000 or 2,500 calorie diet, while others (cholesterol and sodium) remain the same for both calorie amounts.

What's On The Nutrition Facts Label 2

Appendix A | Worksheets

Nutrients

The Nutrition Facts Label can help you learn about the **nutrient content** of many foods in your diet. It also enables you to compare foods to make healthy choices.

The Nutrition Facts Label must list: total fat, saturated fat, *trans* fat, cholesterol, sodium, total carbohydrate, dietary fiber, sugars, protein, vitamin A, vitamin C, calcium, and iron.

The Nutrition Facts Label may also list: monounsaturated fat, polyunsaturated fat, soluble fiber, insoluble fiber, sugar alcohol, other carbohydrate, vitamins (such as biotin, folate, niacin, riboflavin, pantothenic acid, thiamin, vitamin B_6, vitamin B_{12}, vitamin D, vitamin E, and vitamin K) and minerals (such as chromium, copper, iodine, magnesium, manganese, molybdenum, phosphorus, potassium, selenium, and zinc).

Nutrients to get less of – get less than 100% DV of these each day: saturated fat, *trans* fat, cholesterol, and sodium. (Note: *trans* fat has no %DV, so use the amount of grams as a guide)

Nutrients to get more of – get 100% DV of these on most days: dietary fiber, vitamin A, vitamin C, calcium, and iron.

Nutrition Facts
Serving Size 1 package (272g)
Servings Per Container 1

Amount Per Serving	
Calories 300	Calories from Fat 45

	% Daily Value*
Total Fat 5g	8%
Saturated Fat 1.5g	8%
Trans Fat 0g	
Cholesterol 30mg	10%
Sodium 430mg	18%
Total Carbohydrate 55g	18%
Dietary Fiber 6g	24%
Sugars 23g	
Protein 14g	
Vitamin A	80%
Vitamin C	35%
Calcium	6%
Iron	15%

* Percent Daily Values are based on a 2,000 calorie diet. Your Daily Values may be higher or lower depending on your calorie needs:

		Calories:	2,000	2,500
Total Fat		Less than	65g	80g
Saturated Fat		Less than	20g	25g
Cholesterol		Less than	300mg	300mg
Sodium		Less than	2,400mg	2,400mg
Total Carbohydrate			300g	375g
Dietary Fiber			25g	30g

Ingredient List

The Ingredient List shows each ingredient in a food by its **common or usual name in descending order** by weight. So, the ingredient with the greatest contribution to the product weight is listed first, and the ingredient contributing the least by weight is listed last. The ingredient list is usually located near the name of the food's manufacturer and often below the Nutrition Facts Label.

Use this list to find out whether a food or beverage contains ingredients that are sources of nutrients you want to get less of, such as saturated fat (like shortening), *trans* fat (like partially hydrogenated oils), and added sugars (like syrups) – and sources of nutrients you want to get more of, such as whole grains (like whole oats).

INGREDIENTS: WHOLE WHEAT PASTA (WATER, WHOLE WHEAT FLOUR), COOKED WHITE MEAT CHICKEN (WHITE MEAT CHICKEN, WATER, MODIFIED TAPIOCA STARCH, CHICKEN FLAVOR [DRIED CHICKEN BROTH, CHICKEN POWDER, NATURAL FLAVOR], CARRAGEENAN, WHEY PROTEIN CONCENTRATE, SOYBEAN OIL, CORN SYRUP SOLIDS, SODIUM PHOSPHATE, SALT), WATER, CARROTS, GREEN BEANS, APPLE JUICE CONCENTRATE, DRIED CRANBERRIES (CRANBERRIES, SUGAR, SUNFLOWER OIL), APPLES (APPLES, CITRIC ACID, SALT, WATER), CONTAINS 2% OR LESS OF: BUTTER (CREAM, SALT), MODIFIED CORNSTARCH, CHICKEN BROTH, ORANGE JUICE CONCENTRATE, APPLE CIDER VINEGAR, SUGAR, SOYBEAN OIL, SEA SALT, GINGER PUREE (GINGER, WATER, CITRIC ACID), YEAST EXTRACT, SPICES, LEMON JUICE CONCENTRATE, CITRIC ACID.

What's On The Nutrition Facts Label 3

Sample label for Macaroni & Cheese

Nutrition Facts

(1) **Start Here** →
Serving Size 1 cup (228g)
Servings Per Container 2

Amount Per Serving

(2) **Check Calories**
Calories 250   Calories from Fat 110

% Daily Value*   (6)

(3) **Limit these Nutrients**
Total Fat 12g	18%
Saturated Fat 3g	15%
Trans Fat 3g	
Cholesterol 30mg	10%
Sodium 470mg	20%
Total Carbohydrate 31g	10%
Dietary Fiber 0g	0%
Sugars 5g	
Protein 5g	

Quick Guide to % DV

• 5% or less is Low

• 20% or more is High

(4) **Get Enough of these Nutrients**
Vitamin A	4%
Vitamin C	2%
Calcium	20%
Iron	4%

(5) **Footnote**

* Percent Daily Values are based on a 2,000 calorie diet. Your Daily Values may be higher or lower depending on your calorie needs.

	Calories:	2,000	2,500
Total Fat	Less than	65g	80g
Sat Fat	Less than	20g	25g
Cholesterol	Less than	300mg	300mg
Sodium	Less than	2,400mg	2,400mg
Total Carbohydrate		300g	375g
Dietary Fiber		25g	30g

Appendix A | Worksheets

Exercise Goal Setting Worksheet

NAME _____ GOAL START DATE _____

My Exercise Goal is: _____
_____
_____
_____

Goal Completion Date: _____

I will know I have reached my goal because: _____
_____
_____
_____

Three things that will help me reach my goal:

1 _____

2 _____

3 _____

Two people who can help me reach my goal:

1 _____

2 _____

Steps to reaching my goal: _____
_____
_____
_____
_____
_____

Relaxation Goal Setting Worksheet

NAME _____ GOAL START DATE _____

My Relaxation Goal is: _____

_____

_____

_____

Goal Completion Date: _____

I will know I have reached my goal because: _____

_____

_____

_____

Three things that will help me reach my goal:

1 _____

2 _____

3 _____

Two people who can help me reach my goal:

1 _____

2 _____

Steps to reaching my goal: _____

_____

_____

_____

_____

_____

Recreation Goal Setting Worksheet

NAME _____ GOAL START DATE _____

My Recreation Goal is: _____

_____

_____

_____

Goal Completion Date: _____

I will know I have reached my goal because: _____

_____

_____

_____

Three things that will help me reach my goal:

1 _____

2 _____

3 _____

Two people who can help me reach my goal:

1 _____

2 _____

Steps to reaching my goal: _____

_____

_____

_____

_____

Relationship Goal Setting Worksheet

NAME _____ GOAL START DATE _____

My Relationship Goal is: _____

_____

_____

_____

Goal Completion Date: _____

I will know I have reached my goal because: _____

_____

_____

_____

Three things that will help me reach my goal:

1 _____

2 _____

3 _____

Two people who can help me reach my goal:

1 _____

2 _____

Steps to reaching my goal: _____

_____

_____

_____

_____

_____

Nature Goal Setting Worksheet

NAME _____ GOAL START DATE _____

My Nature Goal is: _____
_____
_____
_____

Goal Completion Date: _____

I will know I have reached my goal because: _____
_____
_____
_____

Three things that will help me reach my goal:

1 _____

2 _____

3 _____

Two people who can help me reach my goal:

1 _____

2 _____

Steps to reaching my goal: _____
_____
_____
_____
_____
_____

Giving Back Worksheet

NAME_____ MONTH/YEAR_____

Date/Time	Helping Act	For Whom	Where	How I Felt

Monthly Community Service Commitments

NAME _____ DATE _____

Ways I Currently Help Others	Frequency (Daily, Monthly; Hours)

I am currently not helping others because _____
_____
_____
_____
_____
_____

Spirituality Goal Setting Worksheet

NAME _____ GOAL START DATE _____

My Spirituality Goal is: _____

_____

_____

_____

Goal Completion Date: _____

I will know I have reached my goal because: _____

_____

_____

_____

Three things that will help me reach my goal:

1 _____

2 _____

3 _____

Two people who can help me reach my goal:

1 _____

2 _____

Steps to reaching my goal: _____

_____

_____

_____

_____

_____

Values Worksheet

To foster spirituality in your lifestyle, examine your own values. Ask yourself:

1. What defines me as a person?

2. What role has religion or spirituality played in my life?

3. What is important to me?

4. How well do my daily activities reflect my values?

5. Do I neglect issues that matter to me because I'm busy spending time on things that matter less?

6. What are my important relationships?

7. What people give me a sense of community?

8. What/who inspires me and gives me hope?

9. What brings me joy?

10. What are my proudest achievements?

CERTIFICATE OF ACHIEVEMENT
THIS ACKNOWLEDGES THAT

Has Successfully Explored and Implemented
8 Ways To Wellbeing For Recovering People

This _____ Day of _____ 20 _____

APPENDIX B
Additional Resources

Please note that the subsequent listings are possibilities for investigation. It is always a good idea to check with your physician, therapist, sponsor, or other consultant before utilizing any of these resources.

Nutrition

Interestingly and unfortunately, nutrition is an area of the *8 Ways* that can become highly political, and where there are often competing sources of information and advice. As a result, I recommend that you begin by watching several documentaries and begin drawing your own conclusions prior to looking for more advice. Please watch the following:

Food. Inc, by Robert Kenner is available on Netflix and ITunes – 1 hour 29 minutes.

Cowspiracy: The Sustainability Secret by Kip Andersen is available on Netflix – 91 minutes.

Super Size Me by Morgan Spurlock is available on ITunes and Netflix – l hour 38 minutes.

The **U.S. Department of Health and Human Services** is a good source of credible information to help you make healthful eating choices. Consult their website at www.hhs.gov.

The **Nutrition Facts Label – Wikipedia** helps you understand the nutrition information panel required on most packaged food in the United States and many other countries. Be sure to learn how to read these labels in order to be able to make good choices.

If you are looking for a 12-Step approach to food/eating issues, contact **Overeaters Anonymous, Food Addicts Anonymous,** or **Eating Disorders Anonymous** by doing a Google search for local meetings and online resources.

Consult with a local **Registered Dietician** or **Nutritionist** for best, individualized advice in this critical and complicated area.

Exercise

Always consult with your doctor or other health care provider prior to beginning an exercise regimen.

The **U.S. Department of Health and Human Services** is an excellent resource for advice on many aspects of exercise and physical activity. Consult their website at www.hhs.gov for a variety of suggestions and recommendations to add appropriate exercise to your daily life.

Local gyms and YMCAs employ certified personal trainers to consult with if you would like a specific, individualized approach to your exercise regimen.

If you have a Smart Phone, consult the App Store for a variety of exercise routines that you may enjoy.

Relaxation

To find **Mindfulness and Meditation** resources, go to www.mindful.org. The University of CA at Los Angeles and The University of CA at San Diego have free 5, 11 and 20 minute mindfulness exercises on this site, as well as lots of helpful information to get you started.

If you have a Smart Phone, there are numerous Apps available for this purpose. *Headspace* and *Calm* are two that are quite popular. Check your App Store to see what appeals to you.

Recreation

The best sources of organized recreation activities can be accessed through your local Parks and Recreation Dept., available in most communities. Community Colleges also, typically, have offerings of recreational activities. Look online for their schedule of activities and choose what suits you. There are typically all sorts of classes available with an activity or interest to appeal to most everyone. Foreign languages, cooking, dancing, ceramics and studio arts, music and hikes are just a few of the typical offerings.

If you are over 55, your local Senior Citizens Center will have recreation activities of all sorts available.

If you want company for recreational activities, go to www.meetup.com to see what's going on in your area. Meet new friends and have fun trying out a new activity.

For a good resource regarding sex and sexuality, *Erotic Intelligence* by Alexandra Katehakis, MFT, is an excellent place to start. Other suggestions for this topic are available from your therapist.

Relationships

Am I in a Healthy Relationships? Nemours Foundation. April 2008. http://www.uwec.edu/counsel/pubs/bhr.htm.

Building Healthy Relationships. University of Wisconsin-Eau Claire Counseling Services. Available at: http://www.uwec.edu/Counsel/pubs/selfhelp/bhr.htm.

Gottman's Relationship Tips 101. The Gottman Institute. http://www.gottman.com/49804/Self-Help-and Tips.html.

Ten Tips for Healthy Relationships. K-State Counseling Services. Kansas State University. http://www.k-state.edu/counseling/topics/relationships/relatn.html.

Self-help books and other publications on **Relationship** fill shelves in the library and bookstore. Go and browse to find what appeals to you.

If you are partnered or married, attend a Marriage Encounter weekend. Go to www.WWME.org for more information.

For general relationship skill building, group therapy is an ideal format. Go to www.agpa.org for a referral in your area, or ask a local psychologist or other mental health professional about available therapy groups.

Time in Nature

Getting outdoors is as simple as walking out your front door and traversing the neighborhood. Most cities have walking and hiking trails, for which your local Parks and Recreation Department can provide a guidebook or maps.

For 10 ideas and resources for reconnecting your family in nature, go to https://gryphandivyrose.com.

Contact local chapters of the Sierra Club, the Nature Conservancy and the Audubon Society for outdoor activities.

For intensive outdoor education, go to www.outwardbound.org

If you are a student and would like college credit for outdoor skills, go to www.nols.edu.

Giving Back

An altruistic spirit and Giving Back can be as simple as donating money to a favorite charity. It can be a contribution of time and/or talent to another person or organization. Your time and resources will dictate Giving Back, but everyone can give/do something.

If you are looking for volunteer activities to participate in, check with your local Volunteer Bureau. They typically have a long list of organizations in need of volunteers, and are happy to match you with a volunteer opportunity. Schools, churches, hospitals, senior centers, libraries, humane societies, and so many other places would love to have your help!

Spirituality

If you are looking for a faith community, that's easy! There are numerous religious organizations in your community. Research the religious tradition that interests you and find out where and when they meet. Try them out.

For some good suggestions on developing spiritual resources, go to https://www.takingcharge.csh.umn.edu.

And, www.mindbodygreen.com.

Your local bookstore and library have loads of books on aspects of spirituality, religion and spiritual development. Go take a look at what they have to offer and choose something that appeals to you.

To view the "8 Ways to Wellbeing for Recovering People" video, visit:
https://drsonneeweedn.com/publications

Leader's Guide

Dear Leader,

You may be a mental health professional leading a group in inpatient or outpatient treatment. Or, you may be working mostly with individuals you are seeing in treatment. Either way, this workbook can be used effectively to guide patients to optimize their mental health.

Likewise, if you are an individual who discovered this workbook and are doing the work on your own, these directions are for you, too.

Always begin at the beginning! Have your patient/client start this process by reading and responding in writing to the Introductory Chapter. This sets the tone and the stage to advance through the subsequent chapters in any order that is desired.

If this is a group enterprise, after the introductory material has been completed and each member has presented their intentions to you or to the group, the *8 Ways* chapters can be done sequentially or in any order chosen by you or group members.

If this is an inpatient or an outpatient group, whereby patients admit in an ongoing basis, have the newly admitted patient read over and complete the introductory material and then join the group in whatever chapter they happen to be working on. The point is that there is no particular order needed or required to addressing the chapters and their activities.

This workbook can be completed as quickly or in as leisurely a manner as your time and schedule permits. However, the main thing is to remind patients that this workbook can be with them for a lifetime, as there are always improvements to be made and areas needing attention to achieve a more balanced lifestyle. The idea is to have good information about optimizing mental health, resilience and wellbeing, and a means of keeping track of progress, continuing to make adjustments to Therapeutic Lifestyle Changes as needed.

Feel free to add other materials, amplify what has been provided, and in any other way teach and ground the material offered here.

Here's to a vibrant and healthy life!

Sonnee D. Weedn, Ph.D.

www.ingramcontent.com/pod-product-compliance
Lightning Source LLC
Chambersburg PA
CBHW081216230426

43666CB00015B/2752